HE KEPT HIS PROMISE,

How do you stand on the Word of God when your legs of FAITH are Broken?

Brandy "*BrandyWine*" Rankins

He Kept His Promise;

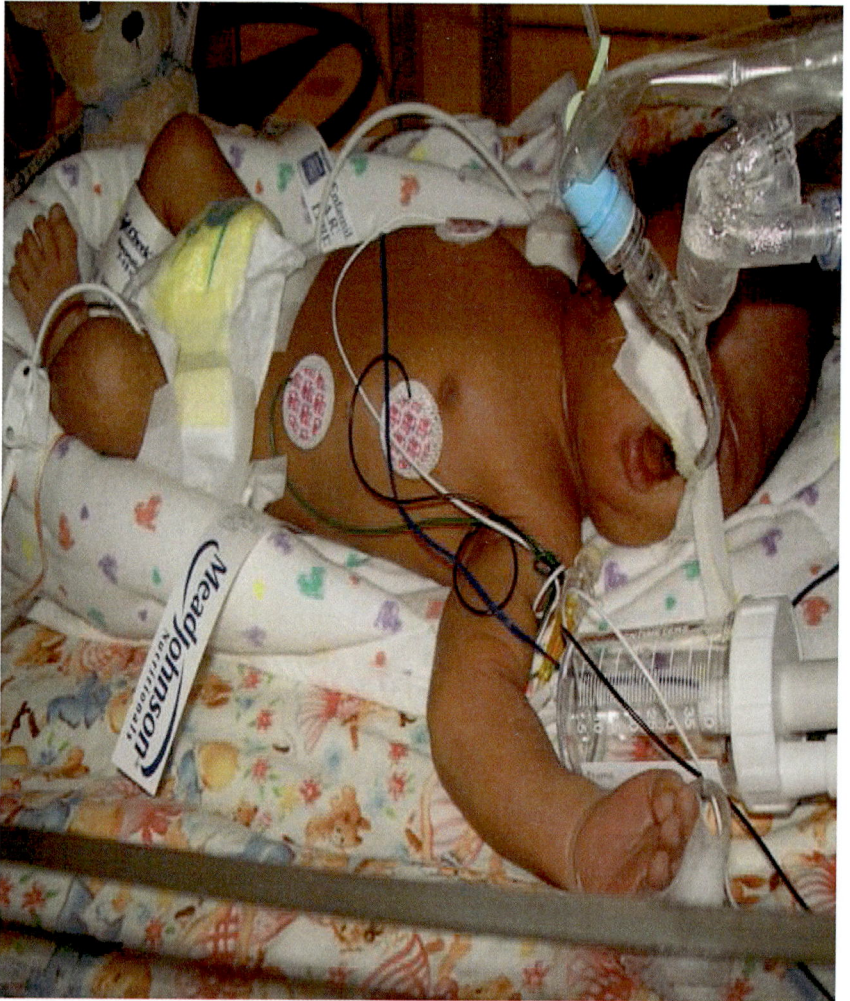

How do you stand on the Word of God
when your legs of FAITH are Broken?

Brandy "BrandyWine" Rankins

He Kept His Promise;

© Copyright 2009- Brandy "*BrandyWine*" Rankins
Cleveland, OH 44137

http://www.freewebs.com/brandywine01

http://www.theredeemedwomen.webs.com

ISBN 978-0-578-03833-9

Cover Design/Graphics: Greater Occasion Designs
Brandy and Thomas Rankins Jr. (216) 269-3504
Saviva1@sbcglobal.net

Author: Brandy "*BrandyWine*" Rankins
Associate Editors: Thomas Rankins Jr. and Kent Poteat
Editor-In-Chief: Brandy "*BrandyWine*" Rankins
For Worldwide Distribution
Printed in the U.S.A.

- 3 -

*How do you stand on the Word of God
when your legs of FAITH are Broken?*

Brandy "BrandyWine" Rankins

He Kept His Promise;

<u>*Blurbs*</u>

"For whomsoever much is given, of him shall much be required...." God has blessed Brandy to go through much in her life; experiences that cause hurt and loneliness and probes the spirit, the intellect and the emotion. Yet through careful obedience and sensitivity to God's voice she stands as a great witness and living testimony to God's faithfulness. Moving forward in God's power she displays the ability to stand on God's promises of healing, restoration and victory in the midst of adversity and how to soar with eagles. I know this book will minister to the hearts of the hurting and hopeless, encouraging them that God is able to do exceedingly, abundantly above all that they ask or even think.
~Lady Linda Lipford, Founding First Lady ~ Zion Pentecostal Church of Christ- Cleve., OH

When times seem the hardest we often loose Faith in God quickly. This book will be great guide on how to remain faithful to God when it seems as if everything in life is going wrong because God always keeps his promise! ~HN(SW) Bobby Gist United States Navy

"When we face really hard times in life, like Job we're tempted to turn inward and sit in despair before God. Brandy has been through the fire of hard times but has chosen to testify to God's sustaining presence and his power for healing. For anyone who needs to be reminded that God is present with us in hard times, but especially for those in the midst of hard times, I believe Brandy's witness to the power of God will be a blessing." ~Pastor Mike Benner Koontz and Waterside Churches of the Brethren- Bedford, PA

- 4 -

*How do you stand on the Word of God
when your legs of FAITH are Broken?*

Brandy "BrandyWine" Rankins

He Kept His Promise will ignite anew the faith of the faint-hearted who are facing what seem to be insurmountable circumstances. Every page reverberates with God's assuring word that indeed faith is the glorious victory that overcomes every destroying arrow of adversity that is hurled at the people of God. You will cry, smile, and rejoice with this gifted and anointed author as she shares her incredible journey of tragedy, healing, and renewal. – Pastor Marilyn Harp, Zion Springs Church- Cleveland, Ohio

Brandy is the essence of an ordinary woman doing extraordinary things. I have witnessed her transition from performing of the world to becoming a change for the world. She has a gift that touches all from listeners to parishioners, from readers to believers. Her words are powerful, yet pure, eloquent reflections of life through testimonial triumph and the struggles we see in today's society. ~Sherman "L.S.Royal" Stewart- writer/poet/emcee

This book will reveal to you that God is real. That faith will bring you thru the toughest of times and once you've weathered the storm the blessings will come.
 ~Leonard "The Answer" Johnson, poet

How do you stand on the Word of God
when your legs of FAITH are Broken?

Brandy "BrandyWine" Rankins

Dedication

Lord, I dedicate this book to you and it is written solely for your glory. I thank you for even giving me the strength to face and speak out about my past and tell my testimony. With all that is within me, I bless you for just being who you are and for sacrificing your life on the cross for me and the entire world.

When it came to restoring my brokenness~ **YOU KEPT YOUR PROMISE**. You told me that night as I was leaving the NICU from seeing Brielle "I brought you back to your place of pain to heal you". I had no idea how much healing I still needed after ten years. You took me back to the same floor of the same hospital where Ramone, my first husband, passed away and healed my daughter Brielle. You know how hard it was for me to return there but you gave me the strength to go. I blamed so many doctors for his death and I vowed to never ever go back to that hospital. I never imagined you would take me back to the place where I gave up…to restore me. When Ramone died I was devastated, when my mother passed away I was hopeless, but when you said YES to Brielle….well there are just no words to describe how amazing it felt that you did that for me; for my family. Even now my only response is tears because I know you heard my prayer and you said yes.

*How do you stand on the Word of God
when your legs of FAITH are Broken?*

Brandy "BrandyWine" Rankins

*I know I will never understand the **"whys"** of my life and, instead of trying to, I just want to be better at saying **"I trust you Lord"** and **"send me, I'll go"**. I never knew telling the truth and sharing my story would be so challenging. I've carried guilt, shame, and insecurities for many years. Writing this book allowed me to cast all those things back to the pit of Hell from which they came. I pray that someone will read this testimony and gain salvation and a new hope in you. You called for me to write this book specifically the way you said and not only required humility and selflessness but most of all trust. I thank you for meeting me in the arc of my testimony just like you said you would.*

To be totally honest, I wanted to give up long ago; I never thought I could make it through what felt like the worst times of my life. Lord you proved me wrong and now I know for myself that with you ALL things truly are possible. I love you Lord and I thank you for first loving me and never letting me go. I have tried to be as transparent as I could between these pages and I pray you are pleased. Many times I have doubted / questioned you, and I have sinned terribly throughout my life, yet you knew my life in advance and still got up on that cross and died for me.

Every time I simply look at Brielle, see her smile, or hold her in my arms I know:

HE KEPT HIS PROMISE!

- 7 -

How do you stand on the Word of God when your legs of FAITH are Broken?

Brandy "BrandyWine" Rankins

How do you stand on the Word of God when your legs of faith are Broken? By having the courage to go back to the place you gave up and allowing God to heal, restore, and show you who HE is for yourself.
*Thank you for healing my legs of faith, teaching me how to stand in the face of adversity, and for bringing restoration to **EVERY** area of brokenness in my life. I love you Father, I bless you, and give you the highest praise. Hallelujah~*

Now Lord throughout the pages of this book as well as my life, I ask that I forever decrease and you INCREASE!

Dr. Oliver Soldes thank you for allowing God to use your hands and give you the knowledge to complete not one but three extraordinary surgeries on Brielle. Your words always increased our faith and constantly prepared us for the next level of the journey we had to travel. I will forever be grateful.

Dr. Kadakkal Radhakrishnan you are an awesome person and a true Godsend.

To: Dr. Jennifer Peterson, Dr. Carmela Lemcke, Dr. Margarita Neyman, Dr. Marita D'Netto, Sarah Keil, Therese Pujolas, Andrina Sabet, Andrea Zjaba and Michelle, Social Workers: Kelly Vitello and Andrea, all the nurses on the NICU floor at Cleveland Clinic Hospital main campus, the Labor & Delivery Staff at Hillcrest Hospital, and all the wonderful doctors, nurses, and staff at the Cleveland Clinic main campus and Children's Rehabilitation Center (Shaker Hts, Campus) We thank you and will always be grateful to you for taking such wonderful care of Brielle Rankins.

A very special thanks to The Ronald McDonald House who change the lives of children and families like Brielle every single day!

How do you stand on the Word of God when your legs of FAITH are Broken?

Brandy "BrandyWine" Rankins

He Kept His Promise;

For
RaShaun, Traci "Chrissy", & Shanita

Just when you feel like you can't
take the wait anymore...

Watch God step in and do something
INCREDIBLE!

B.E.L.I.E.V.E

Because
Emmanuel
Lives
I
Expect
Victory
Everytime

*How do you stand on the Word of God
when your legs of FAITH are Broken?*

Brandy "BrandyWine" Rankins

He Kept His Promise;

Table of Contents

*How do you stand on the Word of God
when your legs of FAITH are Broken?*

Brandy "BrandyWine" Rankins

*How do you stand on the Word of God
when your legs of FAITH are Broken?*

Brandy "BrandyWine" Rankins

How do you stand on the Word of God when your legs of FAITH are Broken?

Brandy "BrandyWine" Rankins

He Kept His Promise;

"There is no greater agony than bearing an untold story inside you"

~ Maya Angelou

{Chapter One}

How do you stand on the Word of God when your legs of FAITH are Broken?

Brandy "BrandyWine" Rankins

Being told that you are going to have a baby is supposed to be one of the happiest times of your life. From the moment you see the two blue lines on the test stick (depending on which pregnancy test you take) you are filled with shock, disbelief, excitement, and anticipation. Even after your OBGYN confirms your pregnancy you, are still thinking *"wow, I am going to have a baby"*. Then you try to imagine what your beautiful planned or unplanned blessing will look like. Your mind can even run rampant wondering what gender your baby will be, whose eyes they will have, and what will labor be like? You begin to just go on and on with the wonder of who this little person will be.

I was 30 weeks into my third pregnancy getting an ultrasound when my husband and I were given the news we were having our first girl. We were so excited! No, we were beyond excited. We were elated, jubilant, overjoyed, thrilled, and just about any other synonym you can think of whose meaning is the same. You see, my husband and I had a blended family, both bringing a son each from previous relationships to our marriage. Together, we gave birth to a wonderful son, giving us three boys. So, finding out that a beautiful princess would be added to the equation was nothing less than an answered prayer from God.

As we sat there discussing all of the possible names for our daughter, we noticed the nurse and doctor standing right outside the opened door talking. From the grimaces on both of their faces, I immediately knew that something wasn't quite right with the ultrasound. The doctor even came back in the room, studied the ultrasound again, nodded his head in disappointment, and then

- 16 -

How do you stand on the Word of God
when your legs of FAITH are Broken?

Brandy "BrandyWine" Rankins

went back into the hallway. Although my husband began encouraging me not to worry so much about something being wrong, I could tell he received the same instant vibe that I did.

I was extremely ill during this pregnancy and many days the constant vomiting, nausea, and restlessness I experienced seemed absolutely unbearable. I even had to go to the emergency room several times because I had gotten so sick. The first time; I found myself repeatedly wheezing, coughing, and in pain when I took a deep breath. As a child, I was diagnosed with asthma and was only affected by it in the winter and when the seasons changed. The rest of the year, I was fine and didn't have to take any medicine. However, this episode occurred at the start of the winter season and my rescue inhaler wasn't helping my constricted airway or tightness I began feeling in my chest.

The ER doctor suggested several steroids but I was reluctant because I was in my first trimester of the pregnancy. I knew how vital the baby's growth was in the first trimester and I wanted to do everything I could to protect that. The doctor got frustrated with me, explaining that if I couldn't breathe the baby couldn't either, and demanded I take the pill. I had already taken steroids through a nebulizer the nurse gave me and was feeling extremely "high". I was firm in protecting my baby so I only pretended to take the high dose steroid pill he gave me. As soon as he exited the room, I spit it out.

Since my first pregnancy I had been considered high risk because I developed toxemia, now called pre-eclampsia, around the 7 month of pregnancy; and the baby, my oldest son, had completely stopped growing. I had endured so many challenges that, on the day I was induced, I had to be put on stroke medicine because my blood pressure had become dangerously high. I tried explaining many times previously to my obstetricians that my body was screaming "something is wrong", but they kept ignoring me by saying I was a hypochondriac. Unfortunately, by the time they actually got to see for themselves that something was wrong, it was almost time for me to deliver.

The first thing I noticed was how I was carrying my son during the pregnancy. My stomach wasn't growing very big and it seemed I carried the extra weight in almost every other part of my body. The job I worked at that time had about six other women that were pregnant and I would compare myself to them and there were things that just didn't add up. I understood that women gained weight and carried differently but, when I was six months pregnant, a woman that was four months pregnant was showing much more than me.

Then the swelling began. I had another friend that was further along in her pregnancy and she was diagnosed with both gestational diabetes and toxemia. Her feet were so swollen at one point that all she could wear was flip flops, and it was dead winter in Cleveland. If you know anything about Cleveland, you know our weather is interchangeable and our winters are extremely cold. It can be 60 degrees one day and 20 degrees the next. So, to see my friend have to wear flip flops in the dead of winter definitely grabbed my attention.

How do you stand on the Word of God
when your legs of FAITH are Broken?

Brandy "BrandyWine" Rankins

A few months later, I noticed my own feet, hands, and face began to swell the same way as hers. The difference was that now it was summertime and, instead of doctors thinking to test me for pre-eclampsia/toxemia, they dismissed my concerns this time by saying it was from the heat. That was until the day I came in and they measured my stomach to find that, at 21 weeks, I was only measuring at 16 weeks. The physician's mouth dropped so hard he almost fell over the table. I presume that he immediately excused himself from the room to gain his composure so that he could handle me if I lost mine. He came back in and measured me three more times with this terrible look of disbelief on his face before he explained what was going on. I just wanted to slap him when he said it. Honestly, that's how frustrated I was with him at that point. *"When I kept trying to tell you something was wrong, you kept telling me I was over reacting, labeling me the worrier, and now you mean to tell me something really was wrong? Where exactly did you go to get your degree in delivering babies?"* These were the words I bit my tongue hard to keep from saying. I just sat there listening with my fist clinched staring down at my horribly swollen feet. Speaking of feet, let's talk about my poor feet for a moment. My feet looked like big ol snausages or something out of the Nutty Professor or Incredible Hulk movies. To make matters worse, no matter how much I put lotion on them, they never ever stayed moisturized, so they were extremely ashy. It was absolutely terrible and, not only were they swollen, but they were cracked too!! How embarrassing!

The pregnancy was only half of my troubles. There was the young man I was pregnant by. His name was LC and, like me, he

- 19 -

was a performance poet that I met at a local spoken word venue I used to frequent. He stood about 2 inches taller than me and was about three years older. For the most part, he seemed to be exceptionally sociable and intellectual, and I enjoyed his poetry. He performed a lot of romantic pieces and it wasn't long before he became popular with the ladies. While performing most of his poems, he'd do things like randomly select a lady from the audience and serenade her with roses and/or chocolates. He told a lot of jokes and a lot of times after the venue I would find myself standing outside conversing with him and other poets.

I met LC while I was in a relationship with a guy named Jamaal. I met Jamaal at a mutual friend's birthday party and I was simply in awe with how attractive he was. He was about six feet tall, light skinned with freckles, and his body was tremendously conditioned. His shirt loudly advertised his six-pack and his smile had me giggling like a school girl. He didn't waste any time telling me he had three children by three different women and, instead of the sirens and lights going off telling me to run, I gave him my phone number.

By the time I met Jamaal, LC and I had been dating for about 16 months. Initially, LC and I were only friends and he was even in a relationship. The more LC and I hung out and talked, it became obvious that neither one of us were happy in our relationships. In my mind, Jamaal was super fine and, while bragging about that made me feel confident, in the end it simply wasn't enough. He never came out to the poetry venues to support me and he never took me out to dinner, or any public setting for that matter.

Honestly, he never really took the time to show me he was interested in me as a person. Most of his time was consumed with working out at the gym and playing football. His obsession with his physical appearance had taken the place of any quality time with me, and I was just about fed up with it. I would find myself settling big time just to be in a relationship with a guy that was quote UN quote *fine*. I wasn't saved at the time so I was intimate with Jamaal, and it only added to the emptiness I felt in the relationship.

Meanwhile, LC always found the time to hang out, shop, or go out to dinner with me. I really loved his personality, yet I wasn't attracted to him physically. I talked to my closest friends about this on several occasions because I felt torn between the two. I used to always say, if I could take LC's personality and put it inside of Jamaal's body, I would have the perfect mate. "Bran, you got a man who is willing to spend all his time with you and go shoe shopping with you girl and you sitting up here wondering what you should do", my first friend stated. "It's obvious that he likes you and he's not ashamed to let everyone know it", she continued. *"And that sorry Jamaal… girl please! Looks ain't everything; everyone sees how he treats you. You better get with someone who's gonna appreciate you, not somebody who thinks they look better than you"*, my second friend laughed. "You suppose to like someone for their personality anyway. *So what he's not your type? His inside will outshine that outside anyway. Girl, just think about it, would you rather stay unhappy in a relationship with someone you barely see because he's fine, or date someone who's truly into you for you"*, she finished. ***BIG SIGH*** *"Yeah ya'll right"*, I agreed. *"I just don't see LC like that"*, I said before shrugging my shoulders.

- 21 -

He Kept His Promise;

About two months later, I decided to break up with Jamaal. I got fed up with his lack of everything in the relationship and I knew I deserved better. I even told him I deserved better when I broke up with him, in addition to some not so nice words I yelled at him. He wasn't moved. "Other people", he scoffed. "Yeah, okay and when you done with your little venture you'll be right back with me. You need to think about what you're doing cuz I ain't gone be waiting on you long", he finished. *CLICK* I hung up the phone on him completely in disbelief and disgust from his arrogance.

While I didn't plan it that way, less than one month later, I was seeing LC. I would always use the excuse "I'm not ready for a relationship" as a means to avoid a commitment with him. I wanted to just have fun with him and I began to experience what it felt like to be the center of someone else's world. I even tried to date other people, but in time LC kept it no secret that he was not willing to share me with anyone.

It wasn't long before I became intimate with LC. I knew this entire thing with him had gone too far but I couldn't help myself or, should I say, I didn't know *how* to help myself. LC had invited me on a trip to Atlanta with him. I had never been on a plane and was absolutely terrified. I told him in the past how I had never flown and how it was a fear I needed to overcome; so, I was definitely impressed when he presented me with a paid for plane ticket at the time of his invitation.

Needless to say, I went on the trip to Atlanta with him. I cried and hyperventilated the entire plane ride, but I made it. Two weeks

*How do you stand on the Word of God
when your legs of FAITH are Broken?*

Brandy "BrandyWine" Rankins

after I returned home I became very sick, and it never crossed my mind that I was pregnant. I was extremely shaken by the news from the positive pregnancy test I took. Immediately, I was filled heavily with disappointment. I wasn't in love with LC and I didn't think it was fair to him or me to have a child together. In my eyes, I was just "enjoying the advantages" for once of a man really being into me, and now my irresponsible mindset and actions had come back to bite me in the butt.

When I told LC about the positive pregnancy test, he was ecstatic. He went on and on with promises and vows of taking care of the baby "no matter what". I told him that I was considering an abortion and he immediately cut me off with "*the only option we have is to take care of our child*". As you can imagine, I didn't at all feel the same way. I began calling abortion clinics and looking in the paper for price quotes. It wasn't long before I totally made up my mind that I was going to get an abortion and completely walk away from LC.

I had just left and friends house and was driving home one night. I didn't have the radio on because the thoughts of getting the abortion were playing in my mind loud enough. I was just about to arrive at my house when I heard a voice softly say "*Mommy you are going to kill me*". I slammed on the brakes and, just as my heart began to race faster, I heard it again. That voice was coming from inside of me, but how? I immediately put my hands on my stomach and began to sob right there in the middle of the street. "*No baby, I could never kill you*", I said. And that was the moment I decided to be accountable for my pregnancy.

How do you stand on the Word of God
when your legs of FAITH are Broken?

Brandy "BrandyWine" Rankins

At the beginning of the pregnancy, LC was more than supportive. He came by daily and eventually moved in temporarily. I had just gotten laid off my job and was collecting severance pay. LC didn't help me financially with the bills but he started cooking, washing my dishes, and doing other chores around the house to help me out. I think that's when I decided to go ahead and make a commitment with him. "It's not like I really have a choice anyway now that I'm pregnant", I thought.

Somewhere around my fifth month of pregnancy things began to change. Not realizing I was in the early stages of toxemia, I began gaining lots of weight and experiencing a lot of sickness. I was never full and I was also experiencing contractions. The more I changed physically, the more LC distanced himself from me. For instance, he would say he'd be over at 8 and wouldn't arrive until 11, which later led to him not arriving at all. One night, I stayed over his mom's house and slept on the floor. LC didn't know I was awake and I overheard him on the phone with a female, making plans to go out to dinner. I was furious and I immediately broke up with him. It wasn't until later in life that I realized me not being physically attracted to him but still dating him for his personality was just as bad as him not wanting to date me because my physical appearance had changed drastically.

When I reached my ninth month of pregnancy I had gained a total of 50 lbs and was extremely swollen. Remember, back in my seventh month they found out my son had stopped growing and immediately began sending me to numerous specialists. The

How do you stand on the Word of God
when your legs of FAITH are Broken?

Brandy "BrandyWine" Rankins

specialists could not find a medical reason as to why he had stopped growing and my obstetrician decided to prematurely induce my labor before I ran into any complications.

I arrived at 5am to the hospital for my induction. My mom and very first friend, Antonise, was by my side. Nissay (as we called her) and I became friends when we were four years old in kindergarten. She had gone to Lamaze classes with me and had prepared to help me through labor in the event LC didn't show up. By this point, LC and I rarely communicated and, while he knew I was having complications with the baby's growth and toxemia, he rarely made it to my doctor's appointments. Initially, I was disappointed but, within a short time, I got over it; however, his mom was extremely supportive and called to check on me often.

They gave me a medicine called patosum to induce my labor. LC was there but he barely said two words to me and spent most of his time in the waiting area. The other medicine they gave me for my blood pressure made me very uncomfortable and unable to complete my sentences, this had me very agitated and anxious. My mom kept encouraging me to relax but, the more I tried, the more I felt out of control, and the higher my pressure became. They even gave me an epidural in an attempt to bring my pressure down, but it did nothing for either my pressure or the unbearable pain. The doctors had me on stand-by for a C-Section because of how high my blood pressure was and how long it remained that way. Before they made a final decision to take me down for a C-Section, I dilated to ten centimeters and was ready to deliver.

- 25 -

How do you stand on the Word of God
when your legs of FAITH are Broken?

Brandy "BrandyWine" Rankins

He Kept His Promise;

Eleven hours later, at 10:48 pm on August 7, 2003, I gave birth to my first son Jah'Mir. He was so beautiful, so precious, and so perfect. He was 5lbs 5ozs and as his eyes stared into mine. I promised to do everything I could to protect, nurture, and love him. It was at that exact moment I had the revelation that I would be raising Jah`Mir all by myself. LC and I argued most of my hospital stay and I also realized I didn't know him at all. It was either that or I didn't take the time to really get to know who he was, more than likely the latter. Either way, it was too late.

I did a lot of thinking over the next few weeks. During my postpartum, most of the swelling and water weight came off of me almost immediately. My blood pressure was still high and would remain that way for a few months, so I had to be placed on medication. Would you believe once that weight started coming off of me LC wanted to get back with me? What's worse is that he had the nerve to come to me and say it. To pour more salt in the wound, he approached me as if nothing happened. He was just like "*I was tripping but now we can be a family*". "**Yeah right on what planet?**" I said. If he could totally abandon me when I was only pregnant, what would he do if, God forbid, it was cancer or worse? There was no way I would commit to someone who showed they thought so small of me.

When I told him I would never get back together with him, he decided to move to New York. He upped and left just like that. He said "*how could I ever tell my son to follow his dreams if I didn't follow my own?*" What a crock of bull! His logic was totally irrational to me and I was appalled by his actions. Anger couldn't

- 26 -

How do you stand on the Word of God
when your legs of FAITH are Broken?

Brandy "BrandyWine" Rankins

begin to describe how I felt seeing him abandon our son like that. I even argued with him and tried persuading him to stay for Jah'Mir, but finally I realized his leaving was for the best. There was no way I could make a man desire to be a father to his son, and I or anyone else shouldn't have to try. A close friend told me "how do you expect him to teach your son how to be a man when he isn't one himself?" Still, to this day, those harsh words echo in my mind.

Over the next several years, LC would rarely come to Cleveland to visit Jah'Mir. His visits would be limited to some holidays and birthdays and, as Jah'Mir got older, phone calls came in every blue moon. Once LC got the news that I was engaged, and seen for himself the time and love my husband, Thomas Rankins Jr., put in with Jah'Mir, he immediately filed papers for joint custody. The process was long and drawn out and I have always felt like it was a spiteful move against me for moving on.

I was 25 then and being a single parent made me very humble and compassionate for those in my shoes. I would know what it meant to face termination from a job for being within the 90 day probation period and taking off work because my son was too ill to attend daycare. I knew the stress of what it meant to worry about enough money to pay rent, bills, buy groceries, and daycare. I had to be the only breadwinner for my household and rarely got a break from raising my son to even know what a babysitter was, or have any "me" time. My mom would relieve me for important appointments, but never to party. I had to grow up and accept responsibility for my son. I was just disappointed that I had to do it alone, since I didn't lie down and make him alone. My mother

*How do you stand on the Word of God
when your legs of FAITH are Broken?*

Brandy "BrandyWine" Rankins

always taught her children to be responsible, especially in the event we became parents. She constantly explained that, once we had children, the freedom we experienced in our lives would be over.

Despite our journey, I have finally learned to forgive LC. Jah'Mir is one of the BLESSED things that ever happened to me. If LC brought nothing else, he brought Jah`Mir, and so his mission is complete. I look back on it all now and I had to take accountability for my part and move on with my life. God never told me that LC was my husband, and I had no business playing dating games with him, let alone having unprotected sex. The Bible talks about being evenly yoked and I knew from the beginning that LC wasn't equally yoked with me, him or Jamaal for that matter.

I struggled with not being physically attracted to him. I believe that, when GOD gives you your mate, they will be all that you desire and need, period. I also believe many of those challenges I faced were a direct result of being unsaved and not knowing God. I had a God-sized void that only God could fill and I almost destroyed myself trying to fill it with worldly measures. Amongst many other things, I was having pre-marital sex in relationships with men as a result of the brokenness I never dealt with, and insecurity of being alone. I know my son is a *PERFECT* blessing from God and the act of sex before marriage was the sin, not him. Many of the challenges I faced and still face today are a direct result of my poor choices back then. Child support payments not being made, "*you said you were coming at 5 and its 9*", buying toys when he really needs clothes and school fees paid, and wiping away my baby's tears because you broke a promise…the list goes on and on.

How do you stand on the Word of God
when your legs of FAITH are Broken?

Brandy "BrandyWine" Rankins

He Kept His Promise;

Jah`Mir is 6 yrs. old now and, while he'll tell you he is blessed with two fathers, he will also tell you he only has one dad, and he knows the difference. He knows that a dad takes accountability for his children, providing daily for them mentally, physically, spiritually, and emotionally. That boy is so intelligent and full of conversation and personality. Ultimately, he will tell you that he will not have children until he is married, gets his college degree, and like his dad Thomas Rankins Jr.; he is going to be in the lives of his children daily.

How do you stand on the Word of God when your legs of FAITH are Broken?

Brandy "BrandyWine" Rankins

He Kept His Promise;

How do you stand on the Word of God
when your legs of FAITH are Broken?

Brandy "BrandyWine" Rankins

Always remember "WHERE" God brought you from

{Chapter Two}

*How do you stand on the Word of God
when your legs of FAITH are Broken?*

Brandy "BrandyWine" Rankins

He Kept His Promise;

On August 27, 1999 at approximately 5pm, at the age of 21, I became a widow. After battling four and a half years with Ewing's Sarcoma, a childhood bone cancer, my first husband, Ramone, passed away. He stood about 5'9" and drastically dropped from 165lbs to 98lbs the day he passed away. He had the disease when we met back in high school but didn't know it. In fact, every time he went to the hospital about the pain they would tell him it was only a hernia and send him back home with medication. He went through this process for most of the first year we dated. Ramone had a lump in his groin and, when it got to be extremely painful, he could barely walk or stand. It wasn't until the latter portion of that first year we dated that we received a diagnosis which stated the lump was cancer. He was admitted into the hospital because, in addition to the pain, he was now unable to use the bathroom. Whenever he was able to go to the bathroom, he was unable fully relieve himself of his bowel and urine. Of course I never thought it was something as serious as cancer, so when he told me he was unable to release all of his bowels, I gave him laxatives. In the beginning, the laxatives gave him comfort, but soon after it only added to the discomfort he was feeling.

An MRI and Cat-Scan revealed he was unable to use the restroom because a tumor as large as a cantaloupe sat on his bowels and bladder and ran down his thigh to his right knee. It was at that point the doctors gave him six months to live. Ramone outlived that prognosis and would go through the next four years receiving chemotherapy and radiation treatments. Initially, the tumor shrank from the size of a cantaloupe to a golf ball. You couldn't even tell he had cancer after his first year of treatments

- 32 -

*How do you stand on the Word of God
when your legs of FAITH are Broken?*

Brandy "BrandyWine" Rankins

because the hair on his head and eyebrows stopped falling out and he began maintaining a healthy weight. Watching Ramone battle that disease was one of the hardest things I've ever done. He received chemotherapy for six days each month and would be very sick during those days of treatment and the days following. He would vomit, have a loss of appetite, dizziness, hair loss, and you could literally smell the chemo coming out of his pores. The scent of chemotherapy is hard to describe and some may dispute there is an odor that comes from the person taking it at all. However, I smelled it and it became more familiar to me when I was around someone being treated with it. Ramone said many times he could smell it also and described it as a "funny chemical smell."

Ramone was so fragile during the times he was receiving treatments. When his treatments for the month were completed, he went through a period of being "neutropenic". Neutropenia is a hematological disorder characterized by an abnormally low number of a type of white blood cell called a neutrophil. Neutrophils usually make up 50-70% of circulating white blood cells and serve as the primary defense against infections by destroying bacteria in the blood. Hence, patients with neutropenia are more susceptible to bacterial infections and, without prompt medical attention, the condition may become life-threatening (neutropenic sepsis) (http://en.wikipedia.org/wiki/Neutropenia).

I would spend many days feeling helpless and guilty as I sat by his bedside. Seeing him suffer that way made me wish I could remove all the pain but I knew I couldn't. Instead, I would just sit there and encourage him from the sidelines with words, drawings, scriptures and anything I could find that was uplifting. On the worst of days he didn't want to hear anything, after all he was only sixteen and a half when he got diagnosed with cancer. During his times of frustration and irritation, he would rant, rave, scream, and break appliances. I couldn't stand to watch him break down uncontrollably into tears. He always asked "WHY" God was letting this horrible sickness happen to him. He would say "Am I terrible person? Did I do something wrong?" He just couldn't understand why he had to endure this kind of illness.

The hospital stays were also very challenging. He was admitted on a pediatric floor. There were children as young as two years old. Some couldn't even walk and were connected to I.V poles and had alopecia (hair loss). Most shared a cancer diagnosis like him, or a disease worse. It was extremely difficult to witness this and not have the answers he and I both desperately needed during that season of our life. Many days I would have breakdowns too. However, I always felt as if I had to hide mine. I felt like I had to be strong for him and, to me, that meant never letting him see me cry or be weak about the situation. I believed if he saw me weak he would give up, and that was just something I couldn't imagine.

Ramone was full of life. It's challenging to try and fully describe his personality for I'm afraid I may leave a single detail out that was significant to his person. First, I would have to say that he was warm, charming, gentle, and kind. His smile was radiant; and one of the things I loved about him most. He was loyal and if you ever got to befriend him you knew it. You knew no matter what happened you could always count on Ramone to be right there by

How do you stand on the Word of God when your legs of FAITH are Broken?

Brandy "BrandyWine" Rankins

your side when you needed him most. And man was he funny! I don't mean just funny like crack jokes all the time funny, but he knew how to make you laugh the times you didn't want to; you know those times, the ones when you've batted your best, yet life pitches you the hardest blows of disappointment, grief, and loss. Well those were the times where he managed to slip right in and bring some of the biggest smiles to your face just when you were convinced you no longer had a smile left to give.

He loved going to parties, amusement parks, and being the life of family gatherings. Most of all, he had the spirit of God in him. There was absolutely no doubt about the fact that God lived in him long before he even knew it himself. He loved just like he laughed...hard. He knew how to encourage people regardless of their trial; always sacrificing for others. He was the biggest male influence and role model to the male youth in his family, and his family and friends as a whole. Many times he was the "go to" person for people to borrow money to help pay their bills, or simply for advice. These were just a few of the qualities he held that made him loved by so many.

When I first met him, he ran the streets, sold drugs, skipped school, and fought a lot.   But when I really got to know him, I found out he was skipping school most of the time to alternate a babysitting schedule of his older sister's three children so that she could attend school. They didn't have any healthcare and babysitting costs at that time was unaffordable for them, so Ramone would stay home from school and watch the children. I

How do you stand on the Word of God
when your legs of FAITH are Broken?

Brandy "BrandyWine" Rankins

admired his sacrifice for children he didn't even birth. What stood out more is that I never saw him complain about doing it.

   One of the things I immediately liked most about him was the way he took on the financial responsibility in his mother's home when it shouldn't have been his burden. Not that I would promote or condone the act but I saw that he sold drugs as a means to help provide his mother's rent, utilities, and groceries. His mom did have a boyfriend, Jo, but he never secured a full-time job during the four and a half years Ramone and I dated. Jo worked odd jobs here and there but ultimately the financial responsibility of the house had fallen on sixteen year old Ramone.

   Now of course he bought other things with the drug money like cars, clothes, shoes, etc. He also bought me very nice expensive things too. It was fast money that not only spent quickly but came with consequences like continuously hiding from the police, never being able to fully trust anyone, and punishing users when they stole from you. In the end, there was absolutely no excuse to validate Ramone selling drugs-it was wrong, period! Yet, when I began to see the entire picture of his life, I could truly appreciate his character.

   The more our relationship matured, the more I saw him mature also. He knew there was something missing from his life and, no matter how much he tried to fill it with materials or money, he knew he couldn't. We began to talk more frequently about God and having a relationship with Him. One of my sister's invited us to her church and we visited the following Sunday and met her pastor,

Pastor Moore. Pastor Moore was a man wise in the Lord. The more we attended church, the more we learned. It wasn't long before we both made the commitment to get baptized. We both knew in our own way that we needed God's help to get through the storms of life.

Watching Ramone get saved was a powerful moment. Here was this young man who was well known throughout the neighborhood for fighting, selling drugs, and never needing to rely on anybody for anything standing extremely vulnerable and weak before God. *"I can't do it any more on my own",* he said. *"I'm sick, I'm tired, and I need the Lord to save me",* he whimpered before crying publicly in front of the entire church.

It was then that I knew, I mean really knew, that God was moving. I thought back to a phone call several months prior that Ramone made to me while I was visiting my mother. He believed that a woman, which he sold crack to, stole many of his crack rocks which he had secured in a plastic bag. It was worth a lot of money and he wasn't leaving her house without it. He told me he believed it fell out when he was sitting on her couch and asked me to come over. When I arrived, there was a lot of chaos and nosy people standing outside of the woman's house commenting on what was going on. When I got to the woman's door, Ramone signaled me inside with him and a house full of his friends. At first, I tried to diffuse the situation. I called myself pulling the woman, who was only 26 by the way, to the side and asking her to simply give back whatever she stole. Yeah I know it was an extremely naive thing of me to do but the woman had a 4 year old son, who was home, and

I just didn't want to see anything go down in front of him. When my approach didn't work, Ramone let me know that he wanted her beat up, and moments later we started fighting. I initiated it by giving her a mean two-piece that sent her crashing into her stereo set before slamming onto the floor. Then my younger cousin and a friend jumped in the fight. The woman got up swinging and attempted to rush me as we literally tore her living room up; it was absolutely terrible. Meanwhile, the background was filled with cheers and chants as what seemed to be the entire neighborhood came into her house to watch. Our punches then turned to kicking and stomping as we all circled around her as she lay on the floor. Now I know what you're thinking; you're probably saying, Brandy, I can't believe the three of ya'll jumped on that one girl. Yes, unfortunately we did. But before you start feeling sorry for her, let me tell you that she wasn't one bit phased by any of it. She was very strong and everything the three of us dished…she ate it all. Her skin was so tough that our kicks sounded like we were stomping on the concrete. I don't know if it was all the crack she smoked (and I'm not at all being funny) but like I said she was strong; incredible hulk strong. I was fighting that girl with all I had and in most moments I felt like I was fighting for my life. I know adrenaline was pumping through us all but her response just wasn't normal. She should've been laid out and hurt but she just kept getting back up; blood, bruises, and all. And it seemed that each time she got up it was with more power and authority than the last time.

Eventually, her son ran downstairs crying and screaming and that's when we stopped and everyone disbursed. As we exited she began screaming out the door that she was calling the police

*How do you stand on the Word of God
when your legs of FAITH are Broken?*

Brandy "BrandyWine" Rankins

and reporting us all. That was our cue to leave and we all ran out of there without looking back. Thankfully she didn't call the police and I never had to see her again. See, back then I considered myself one of the coolest females you could know. However, when you crossed me or mine, I was going to bring it to you double. I had that "you shot my dog and I'm gonna kill your cat, bird, fish, and everything else in your house" attitude. I didn't go looking for fights but I wasn't going to run from one either and I had no problem with letting you know it. That was my mentality and thought process back then. I didn't know how to walk away from drama and found myself frequently fighting to either prove my loyalty to my friends or to defend my reputation. Instead of turning away from the chaos, I took pleasure in helping bring it.

I was then reminded of another situation Ramone faced. In short, he started off fighting these guys that rushed his neighborhood. It ended with 2 people critically shot and Ramone along with three others in jail. It was in the local newspaper and on the news. The media was wrongfully saying police had all three shooters in custody; identifying Ramone as one of the shooters. Ramone didn't have a gun, so he hadn't shot at anyone. His bail was originally set at $500,000. A lot of money, an excellent attorney, and many months later, Ramone was sentenced to probation. He had priors as a juvenile but the ONLY reason he received probation was because of his cancer. All of his charges were high felonies and the charges were complicated. The court took the charges of Ramone and two other individuals and combined them. So Ramone now had several counts of felonious assault (he pulled out a bat and used it) and three gun charges.

How do you stand on the Word of God when your legs of FAITH are Broken?

Brandy "BrandyWine" Rankins

There was gun powder found on one of the others so the court charged all of them with Ramone's felonious assault and all of them with the gun charges as well. Truly, it felt like an impossible situation for everyone involved.

Ramone's doctors' reported that his cancer was terminal and begged the judge to show mercy with his sentencing, which he eventually granted. Despite Ramone surrendering himself to the police, telling what he did, and practically giving himself the case, many started saying he was a snitch. They thought he had to be a snitch since he didn't go to jail and the other two charged did. Ramone did snitch-**ON HIMSELF** and he was very hurt and disappointed that some were labeling him as such. Of the two critically shot was a young female that Ramone grew up with. He felt terrible about her being shot, as well as his friends being arrested over a fight that was initiated by him. Furthermore, he felt if anyone should be in jail it should be him and, less than two hours after the incident, he was.

So when I saw this man with that reputation standing in the sanctuary before the entire church crying out to God, it pierced me. I had never really seen Ramone cry before that and now he was open and completely vulnerable for God. It wasn't long before I opened my mouth and began crying out to God too. We needed a change in our life and we had just about tried everything else to no avail; now it was time to try God, and we did.

I now realize God allowed these extreme situations to happen to get our attention and show us His grace. There had been times where people have pulled out guns and shot at Ramone and he shot back at them. He and some of his friends had gotten into some of the largest bar fights I had ever seen and I know now it was God's grace that kept us alive. I believe these incidents along with others allowed Ramone to feel rejected, isolated, and reach such a point of brokenness that he fell on his knees to God. And there I was standing right beside him with his hand in mine ready to accept Christ too. I know if we would've continued on that road we were traveling, we would've literally died in the world. I was only twenty, he was nineteen, and no matter how hard we thought we were in these streets, neither of us really wanted to die. Who does?

Soon we had stopped drinking, smoking, going out to clubs/parties, and much more. We began to know what it was like to face ridicule from our peers for making the decision to turn away from sin; especially Ramone. People began downgrading him because he was no longer quick to hang out, drink, stand on the block, or doing many of the things he used to. When we found out what people were saying, we were hurt, but we realized fulfilling our commitment to God was far greater; even if that meant letting people in our life down.

Once God renewed Ramone's mind, Ramone then tried to pass it on to the young men in his family. He worked real hard to keep them from selling drugs, fighting for no reason, cursing, and anything negative that would stunt their destiny. He tried to teach them respect and not to walk in his past footsteps. Most of all, he taught them that a real man doesn't spend his days trying to prove

How do you stand on the Word of God
when your legs of FAITH are Broken?

Brandy "BrandyWine" Rankins

to others he is a man by ignorant actions because his character as a man is revealed in his leadership and the examples he sets. Honestly, it was a blessing just to be able to witness his transition. I saw this boy who blamed God and the world for what he lacked turn into this man who learned to trust God with everything, especially his life. The same man who, in the beginning, questioned if there was a God because of the storms he faced became the man who stood on the word of God, and would pray with you first hand. It was priceless. I knew God was doing some awesome things in his life and I just knew He was going to heal that cancer in Ramone's body, and he would live to tell the world about it.

My sister's church was filled with an older crowd and we loved it! They were so nice to us and looked forward to seeing us each week. Seeing the members there receive us like they did definitely made me feel needed. They sang a lot of older hymns and soulful songs, which taught me how to cry out to God about my problems. It was amazing to me many days how most of the songs addressed how I was feeling or what I was going through in my own life. I would find myself singing those songs when I wasn't even at church. In no time, that church became our church and, in more ways than one, a second home to us. We became close with those in leadership at the church and one minister in particular, Minister Pe, became a mentor to us. We loved being around him and hearing him give a word. We trusted him.

During one of our chemo stays we had a visit from Minister Pe. We were excited to see him and it made us feel good that he would take time out to come to the hospital and visit us. About fifteen minutes into our visit, Minister Pe began to share some things that were on his heart. He began to tell Ramone that it was not God's will for him to take chemotherapy or any other treatments. He told us that we were both going against what God wanted for our lives by receiving the treatment. He also said that God is a healer and, by taking the medicine, we were only making the disease worse and not allowing God to remove it. We didn't know how to respond to this so we just sat quietly and let him speak without interruption. Neither one of us knew enough about God's word to agree or oppose. It was more difficult because we really respected Minister Pe and sat under his teachings at the church for awhile. We were just shocked that he would say such things and then treat us like he was disappointed in us. Worse than that, insinuate that God was disappointed in us. After he left, we sat in silence for awhile. The atmosphere was just too heavy for us to speak right away. We both experienced uneasiness and sadness in our hearts about the things he said. We kept saying to one another that we didn't think we were going against God by taking medicine. We didn't allow the confusion to weigh on us long because shortly after we consulted our Pastor about it.

Our Pastor was a wonderful man of God. We appreciated how he always made time for us, despite the many things he had going on in his life and with the church. His wife was the exact same way and she always greeted us with lots of love that you could tell was genuine. She was the type of woman that was soft spoken yet; her words were filled with power and wisdom when they left her lips. She always talked to me with both care and concern; the same way

I seen her speak to her own daughters, and that made me feel good.

Our Pastor listened carefully as we explained the conversation that took place at the hospital between us and Minister Pe. He then took a moment to clear his throat and rubbed his head in total disbelief before giving us a response. He explained to us that what Minister Pe shared with us was his opinion on medicine and treatment and not the word of God. **"Don't you know God can heal with medicine or without medicine if he chooses because he is God all by himself?"** he said. He then declared in a loud voice "**Children, there is nothing too hard for God and, if it be his will to remove that cancer from your body, then chemotherapy or nothing else can stand in His way**"! He further went on to tell us that the uneasy feeling we experienced during the conversation was the spirit of discernment and that it came from God. Discernment was explained to me as the ability of being able to grasp when something is right or wrong spiritually. I now know that it's an essential element to growth in Christ and a way that the Holy Spirit guides you. Surely what Minister Pe told us was his opinion and not from God.

How do you stand on the Word of God
when your legs of FAITH are Broken?

Brandy "BrandyWine" Rankins

He Kept His Promise;

Without the "TEST" there is no testimony!

{Chapter Three}

*How do you stand on the Word of God
when your legs of FAITH are Broken?*

Brandy "BrandyWine" Rankins

My mom told me she wanted to give me something really special for my wedding and, after a lot of saving, she purchased my dress. Her doing that blessed me so much because my mom had financial challenges of her own to meet but she made me and our wedding her first priority. My mom, Shade we called her, always did things like that though. We called my mother Shade, even her grandkids and friends; because she always joked that she was too young to be a grandma. She was comfortable enough to allow us to call her Shade though her and my dad raised us with a strict discipline and respect. We were taught to always express manners and have compassion for others.

I grew up seeing that my mom always sacrificed for her family and never complained about putting her needs last. She sacrificed her education for her marriage and children. Initially, she had many educational opportunities that took backseat to her marriage. Some of the reasons were low self-esteem and even being criticized and told by others she couldn't do it. As she started having us, and we got up in age, she allowed her dreams to just become antiques that sat on the shelf. I was always saddened to hear her explain it because she wasn't just beautiful but she was intelligent and loyal enough to do absolutely anything!

My mom was one of my very best friends. I don't mean the type of parent who tries to be your friend and not your parent but the kind that is still your parent first as well as your best friend. Not too many people can say that about their mom but, for me, I could say it easily. I could talk to my mom about anything. I don't care how busy she was or what she was doing she always dropped

*How do you stand on the Word of God
when your legs of FAITH are Broken?*

Brandy "BrandyWine" Rankins

everything when I needed her most. I have cried on her shoulders many of days and mom always encouraged me regardless of how poor my choices were or whatever trouble I had gotten myself into. Her love for me and all of her children and family was unconditional. I never had to question whether or not she loved me, even when she got mad at me. However, my mother definitely had a temper and could go there if you pushed her. She was the one that you didn't want to take there because, not only would she go to that place…she would go beyond.

There were times her and my dad used to argue in their room upstairs. The argument could be over and 20 minutes later she would go back to the bottom of the stairs and scream up to him "And another thing…." She would continue doing that until she got all of her point out, and sometimes that could last all night long. In my later years I became the same way. Man, I would get you told so good about everything you did today, yesterday, the day before, and the year before that.

My parents' arguments and fights would make me so nervous. They got physical a few times and I developed terrible panic attacks by age 8 as a result. I even had to go and see a therapist because I became terribly afraid of death and related everything to it. I was always on edge and I began experiencing a lot of anxiety and fear.

Most of my siblings were older than me and were gone during the arguments I experienced. They were out hanging with friends or gone here and there while I was stuck at home with the fighting. Many nights I felt trapped because I wanted to be gone also but I

- 47 -

was too young so I couldn't. Initially, I would feel safe when either of my brothers came home during their arguing because I felt like they could handle things if it got out of control. The truth is that they couldn't. I used to always try and run in-between my mom and dad in an attempt to stop their quarrelling but I was rarely successful. They would threaten each other and break things, so I always feared that one of them would kill the other. I mainly feared my dad hurting my mom because he was much stronger physically and once she got mad she never backed down.

I loved spending time with my Shade. We would shop, go out to eat at different restaurants, and sit and talk about all the current events. There weren't too many things I couldn't tell my mother…except "I'm pregnant" of course. That was a no, no! In my mom's eyes, boys and I didn't mix, no matter how old I was. Even as an adult my mom was a strong believer that the proper order was: education, marriage, and then children. Still when I became pregnant at 24 and told my mom, let's just say she wasn't having it. As you can see I wasn't the one of my mother's children that modeled things in the order she taught. As I became older, and experienced a child and marriage before my degree, I had to learn to be okay with that. My mom always expressed she didn't want to see any of her children face any of the financial struggles she faced in her life. I guess her order was her way of protecting us, especially her daughters, from enduring what she did, and I respected that.

The dress she bought me was beautiful but I decided I wanted it in a size or two smaller. All I could think about or envision was my physical appearance for that day. The stress of caring for Ramone over the years always showed in my weight. It would fluctuate continuously trying to cope with everything I had on my plate. Of course there were some of his family members who showed no mercy and made my weight gain the latest topic at some of their family gatherings. This made some of the younger ones jump in too, making jokes about me being a Buford burger and much more. That ticked me off entirely because I never understood how they could have the nerve to speak about someone in that manner. I was only going on seventeen when my boyfriend was diagnosed with cancer and, four years later, I was doing the best I could. Yes, I gained weight but it's not like I was huge, and I don't say that to put down anyone overweight. I say that to point out that, even with a fifteen pound gain, they spoke behind my back as if I had lost all eating control and didn't have a boyfriend with cancer to solely care for.

About two months before our wedding, Ramone's doctor offered him to take part in an experimental program that showed a nice success rate in Ewing Sarcomas. The program was in Maryland and required that Ramone be off of his current chemotherapy treatments for at least a month to enter. By this point, Ramone had been battling this cancer for four and a half years. He underwent 3 major surgeries on his lungs, along with chemo and radiation. The cancer had spread from his thigh to his lung cavity. The amazing part about all of what he was enduring was that you couldn't even see his sickness majority of the time. His body became so used to the chemotherapy regime that his hair stopped falling out, he didn't get as nauseous, and he was able to maintain a healthy weight.

How do you stand on the Word of God
when your legs of FAITH are Broken?

Brandy "BrandyWine" Rankins

He Kept His Promise;

His doctor explained there would be a great risk in taking Ramone off the chemotherapy treatments. He told us that the tumors that were pretty much dormant while on the medicine could grow, or the cancer could possibly spread somewhere else. The other outlook was that the cancer could do nothing at all and just remain the same size until he took the treatment. I don't think we both realized then how big of a gamble the experimental treatment option was. It just felt like we were running out of alternatives and, in our minds, especially Ramone's, we were going to exhaust them all. We stayed praying for a healing, so we just believed this was an opportunity for God to do just that…so we went for it.

For the first three weeks, there weren't any drastic changes in Ramone's health that we noticed from him being off the chemo. I was careful to make a fuss to him about how he was feeling. I watched his sleeping patterns, eating habits, and I just didn't want to miss a detail. We were so excited about going to Maryland and doing the treatment that we didn't even plan a honeymoon. In fact, our honeymoon plans were just that; go to Maryland and get the treatment. We immediately packed our luggage and had made every possible arrangement on our end to make the trip. As far as any hotel arrangements or facility fees, we were under the impression that the hospital would take full responsibility in handling that. Our family and friends were very excited and we just couldn't wait to get married and go to Maryland.

About two weeks before the wedding, I realized something was extremely wrong. Ramone had an appointment to attend and I drove him downtown to it. As he got out the car, I noticed he

*How do you stand on the Word of God
when your legs of FAITH are Broken?*

Brandy "BrandyWine" Rankins

struggled to simply cross the street. That's when I completely turned toward him and placed my hand on the door handle in a premature attempt to get out and help him. Yet I didn't get out, I froze completely in disbelief as I saw him struggling for air as he climbed the flight of stairs to the building. He walked slowly up the stairs and paused about every three to breathe. About half way up the stairs, he was completely bent over and out of breath. All I could do was sit there with my mouth open hurting to help him. The more I looked at him, the more I realized his condition had grown worse. I could see now that his face was sunken in from weight loss. More so, I had never seen him struggle like this to simply breathe while walking or climbing stairs. The shock that came over me suddenly turned into a horrible pain of heartbreak and fear; immediately I broke down sobbing. "This isn't fair God", I shouted in the parked car. Then I began beating my hands on the steering wheel in frustration because Maryland just seemed to be our last hope and it felt like now we weren't going to make it.

The more I cried, the more my mind wrapped itself around the thought that Ramone was dying. Those tears couldn't even symbolize the hurt that thought brought to my being. I just kept screaming out to God "why" and "help us Lord', won't you help us". I began feeling overwhelmed with the many emotions that began to pour out of me in those moments. I felt like I was going to faint, or worse, because I didn't know how to process the fear, sadness, and anger I was experiencing. More than ever, I felt so alone because I couldn't even share my feelings with Ramone. I didn't want to scare or stress him more than he already was. We had come so far and completely changed our lives for God. I just

How do you stand on the Word of God
when your legs of FAITH are Broken?

Brandy "BrandyWine" Rankins

couldn't understand why He was letting this happen. I think that's the part that frustrated me most because, as desperately as I wanted God to change the situation to the way I wanted it, He didn't. About fifteen minutes later I fixed my hair and began getting myself together. I looked out the window and noticed people staring intensely at me as they walked by my car. Many of them laughed and bucked their eyes as if to say "what's wrong with you", but the last thing I cared about in that moment was what people thought. I just knew that the only person who could help was God...and right now He felt so very far away.

*How do you stand on the Word of God
when your legs of FAITH are Broken?*

Brandy "BrandyWine" Rankins

He Kept His Promise;

You expect me to wear "WHAT" down the aisle?!?

{Chapter Four}

How do you stand on the Word of God when your legs of FAITH are Broken?

Brandy "BrandyWine" Rankins

Less than a week before the wedding, Ramone had to be admitted into the hospital again. His doctor said he was dehydrated and needed some additional medication. That had to be one of the most challenging weeks we had faced. Ramone and I were paying for the wedding ourselves and had no wedding planner; this meant we were the wedding planners. So, although Ramone was in the hospital, I still had so much to do in order to have things prepared for the ceremony. Of course this made Ramone grouchy. He knew I needed to do the legwork for the wedding but he wanted me to remain at the hospital with him. In over four years, this was the first time that I didn't stay at the hospital all day and night with him. He never said it but I'm sure that made him anxious in a way of its own. It was a burden on me because, not only did I have to deal with Ramone's attitude and the guilt I began to feel from not being at the hospital all day, but I had to the responsibility of getting the wedding together also.

That Wednesday was the cleaning and pick-up for my dress. I picked up my mom early that afternoon and she went with me to pick up the dress. I tried the dress on briefly, they bagged it, and we were out the door. Well, I was almost out the door until my mom wanted a final look at it. She noticed that the beads and sequence were hanging off of the dress and, sad to say, it was ruined from the steam cleaning they did. My mom held the dress up to the manager and explained the conflict but the manager didn't want compromise. My mother looked at her watch, noticed the time, and told the manager we would be right back to deal with the dress issue. You see, it was now past the time scheduled for us to pick up my aunt and cousin, KiKi, from the bus station. They were

- 54 -

coming into town from Illinois for the wedding and my cousin was one of my bridesmaids. We also had to go back to my mom's house and pick up my two sisters because they wanted to see our aunt and cousin as well.

We arrived at the bus station just in time. They were unloading the bus and we took their luggage to my mom's van for loading. The second my sisters and I saw KiKi, we all began hugging, rocking from side to side, and screaming in excitement because we were so happy to see each other. Once everyone loaded up in the van, my mom and I began to explain the intolerable catastrophe with the dress. I expressed how I was more upset about the manager not wanting to do anything to rectify the situation that the dress actually being ruined. I had been going to this shop for months for fittings. My mom paid close to a thousand dollars for this dress and that was a thousand dollars that I knew she didn't really have to spend on a dress for me. You mean to tell me they can't fix my dress?!! It was just absolutely non-sense! By the time I finished expressing my feelings to everyone in the car, I was almost in tears. When I looked at everyone for a response, their angry faces spoke louder than any words. Finally, the tension thickened when one of my sisters eagerly said "aw naw, lets go to that shop!" So instead of the manager initially having two angry women to deal with about my dress, she now had six.

We arrived at the bridal shop and everybody; I mean everybody was ready to get ignorant. We marched in that store and demanded the manager fix my dress now or else! (Yeah that was pretty much before I knew what it meant to live saved-lol). The manager explained that sometimes the dress can be compromised when the steam clean it before giving it to the bride. She further told us that the store was not responsible for this and that the cleaning is done at your own risk. "***Show me that in writing"***, my mother interrupted." ***Because no one explained that to us before we decided to get her dress cleaned.*** *In fact, we were told it needed to be done so that the dress would look its best for my daughter's wedding"*, my mom went on. The manager became nervous and started babbling. She was making no sense at all and all the customers began staring at us and whispering. Meanwhile, KiKi was walking around the store holding up different dresses saying loudly *"Bran Bran, what do you think about this one? Because if they are not going to fix that dress you bought, then they are going to give you a new one!"* *"That's right and you can get any dress up in here you want"*, one of my sisters cut in. *"I know that's right"*, I exclaimed as I began taking the different dresses and trying them on.

There was a beautiful gown in particular that got my attention. The dress my mom bought me was definitely beautiful also but these dresses were complete opposites. My dress had a portrait neck, long sleeves engraved in hearts, and the train was engulfed with three hearts ranking from small to large. This dress was a princess dress. It reminded me of Cinderella. It had spaghetti straps and was heart shaped at the top. The train was full but, instead of being long, it puffed out all around me. I knew instantly this was the dress I wanted.

How do you stand on the Word of God
when your legs of FAITH are Broken?

Brandy "BrandyWine" Rankins

I tried the dress on and fell in love with it. KiKi didn't make it any better because she offered me some gloves to try on as well, and that sealed the deal. Meanwhile, the manager was standing on the stage area where I was trying the dress on saying she could not give me this dress. Actually, it was two managers because she went and got her manager due to how bad we were clowning in her store. So really they both were saying no and that the dress I had on was much more expensive than my dress. They were saying they could exchange the dress but it had to be the exact price. "Hog wash, I'm getting this dress", I pouted under my breath and proceeded to turn around in the mirror looking at myself. "Do you like it Brandy? Is this the one you want", my mom asked impatiently. I nodded a big yes to her. A lot of arguing and a few seconds later I was walking out of the store with my new dress and gloves to match. The only issue now was that I had to have this new dress and train, which was made completely out of layers and layers and layers of chiffon, altered.

The seamstress from bridal shop was more than nice and she offered to alter my dress free of charge. She gave me her number and within the next two days I met her at her house for the alterations. She was only able to alter the dress late in the evening and, being that my wedding was less than 4 days away... I didn't have a choice. I agreed to take whatever opening she gave me and totally respected that I was at the mercy of her time and talent.

When I arrived at her home, she took no time getting started. It was so humid that I couldn't stop sweating and my feet were throbbing from standing in her kitchen while she worked. It took her

How do you stand on the Word of God when your legs of FAITH are Broken?

Brandy "BrandyWine" Rankins

about 3 hours to do everything she needed to do to the dress with me in it. She did her best to pin and sew what she could. I looked at the clock before I left and was disappointed to see that it was going on 2a.m. This would make yet another day that I didn't get up to the hospital to spend any quality time with Ramone.

Beloved, Finally the time has come for us to say "I DO"

{Chapter Five}

He Kept His Promise;

Ramone got released from the hospital the day before our wedding. When I saw him, I could see that he was weak and still not feeling well. His doctors didn't want to discharge him from their care at the hospital, but they did on account of our wedding.

Ramone and I lived in a townhouse adjoined to a really big park and had a cocker spaniel named Passion. All his friends used to come over and crack on Passion saying "out of all the dogs in the world to buy, yall had to go and get a soft, wimpy, and girly dog like a cocker spaniel." But I used to stand up for my dog I loved that dog and I couldn't care less what they were saying about her. Most of them had two and three pit bulls and those types of dogs were just too vicious for me. Don't get me wrong, we definitely had our share of dogs because Ramone also liked the big vicious dogs.

Our first dog was a rottweiler. I can't remember her name but oooooh I did not like that dog; I used to call her a demon dog because of the energy in her eyes. I could tell the feeling was mutual because she made it well known that she didn't like me either. She would just sit for periods completely mean mugging me and doing this low growl as if to say "you try it and I will eat you to pieces". No, I don't speak dog but I got her message loud and clear and never tried petting or approaching her like I do most cute dogs.

One afternoon I recall Ramone putting food and water in her bowl and sitting it on the floor to feed her. He must have forgot to add something, which caused him to pick the bowl back up just as she was about to eat it *BIG MISTAKE*. As he picked the bowl up,

- 60 -

the puppy bit him and snatched a nice size plug from his hand. Of course he spanked the puppy but, still after I saw that...yep I was convinced she was a demon dog and she did not last in our house long.

Then we got a pit bull. She was a puppy and was really pretty for a pit bull anyway. She had blue eyes and I was just amazed at how much she loved cuddling with me. Passion didn't like this and, one day after leaving them two together while I went to run some errands, we were shocked at what we found. Passion had bit a chunk out of the pit's nose. Yep you read right, Passion-the cocker spaniel had bit a chunk out of the pit bull's nose and had it whimpering while backed into a corner. I know what you're thinking because as I sat there with my mouth open I thought the same thing, but I think it happened because the pit was a baby and Passion was a little special herself. She had gotten a hold of some of Ramone's narcotic pain pills one. We had to rush her to the nearest animal hospital and it was very dramatic for me because the doctor wasn't sure if she would make it. She would growl, and then whimper, and it got real bad once she started foaming at the mouth. She was trying to bite me when I tried calling her name and it was just a terrible experience. Needless to say, God brought her through that but she was never the same. She thought she was a pit bull and she was scared of nothing.

I would take Passion for walks after that and she would bark people down that came close to me. She was very protective of me; even towards Ramone. Sometimes he would tickle me to the point that I would fall out laughing and she would bark up a storm.

How do you stand on the Word of God when your legs of FAITH are Broken?

Brandy "BrandyWine" Rankins

One time he was tickling me and she began running around him barking and biting him on different areas of his ankles, causing him to fall. When he hit the ground, she got up in his face barking. He was upset but it was so funny that we couldn't help but laugh about it.

The night before the wedding, Ramone and I decided to sleep in different places to keep us from seeing each other before the wedding. He stayed at our place with his friends and Passion and some of my friends and I stayed at my mom's home. I was up most of the night getting my hair done by one of my sisters so I was completely exhausted when I got in. I know my sister was exhausted also because she did most of the ladies hair from my bridal party too!

Our colors were white, red, and buttercup-which is close to the color gold. Red was his favorite color and gold is mine. I had a matron of honor, a maid of honor, and eight bridesmaids. Likewise Ramone had two best men and eight groomsmen. We then had four or five flower girls and four of our nephews served as ring bearers and bible carriers. My paternal grandmother passed away right before my wedding. My father went to Virginia for her funeral and so my brother Jared walked me down the aisle in his place.

I married Ramone on June 12, 1999. It was an extremely hot yet beautiful day. It was such a surreal moment in my life and one that I could never dream coming to pass. We had some family members and friends who tried to rush us getting married due to his illness but we didn't let that be an issue. I even had a friend of mine family member ask me "Why are you marrying someone who is dying?" I was so upset that she even said that to me and I had several choice words that I wanted to say but, out of respect, I simply answered "because I love him". I thought it was quite ignorant to take a marriage vow to be with someone through sickness and health as long as they were healthy and not if they were ill. **1 Corinthians 13:7** the Amplified version says *"Love bears up under anything and everything that comes, is ever ready to believe the best of every person, its hopes are fadeless under all circumstances, and it endures everything [without weakening]."* It just angered me that people couldn't see that we weathered the storm for four and a half years together and loved each other enough to marry. No opinions, no debates, no judgments-just simply be happy for us and whatever time God granted our marriage.

Standing beside Ramone at the altar was absolutely priceless. After four years I was so thankful to finally be standing in my wedding dress marrying my high school sweetheart and someone I loved dearly. I was also thankful that, even though we had to rent out a separate church for the ceremony, our Pastor was able to perform the service.

The heat had filled the sanctuary and I began sweating excessively. To make it worse, whoever unlocked the church for our ceremony did not turn on the air conditioner or stick around so that we could ask them to. Soon I began taking a special concern for Ramone because I could see the heat was making it hard for him to breathe. I tried not to stare at his chest as it began inflating

How do you stand on the Word of God when your legs of FAITH are Broken?

Brandy "BrandyWine" Rankins

rapidly with short breaths accompanied by wheezes.   Despite the anxiety that began to consume me, I fought back the tears and tried to focus on the wedding.

After the ceremony we drove around for almost 2 hours in our rented stretched expedition, showing off to any and everyone we seen. We honked horns, took turns standing through the sun roof waving, and stopped anywhere we saw a gathering to jump out and take pictures for everyone to witness. We were actually really late arriving to our wedding, so we lost about an hour on the rental because we signed an earlier time on the contract.

When we arrived at the reception, it was beautiful. One of my sisters, my cousin KiKi, and a few of my bridesmaids really did a good job decorating. We rented out a community hall and were responsible for all the decorating ourselves as well. This, in addition to planning the wedding, was no easy task at all. I'm so thankful to my sister and everyone else who helped that day because they had to run on the other side of town to decorate the hall, then get into their dress and make it to the wedding.

The DJ was a guy I went to school with named Tacu and he really did his thing with the music. We received some very nice toasts and had a really special first dance on the floor. Since my dad was in Virginia, I did the father daughter dance with my brother Jared, and I think that had to really be one of the moments that I realized how special he was in my life. Both of my brothers play extremely significant roles in my life but the way my brother Jared

How do you stand on the Word of God
when your legs of FAITH are Broken?

Brandy "BrandyWine" Rankins

took charge and stepped up to be my covering that day was just priceless.

Unfortunately, Ramone sat down during most of the reception. His breathing was fast paced and you could see his chest rise and fall irregularly as he sometimes panted just to get air. His skin was pale and his tuxedo kept no secrets of his weight loss, for it discretely whispered about it to every eye that took notice of the groom. Ramone knew his weight loss was extreme and he was uncomfortable with anyone taking his picture, especially now on his wedding day. I'm sure it only made matters worse that every five minutes I kept asking him if he were okay.

Remembering him from those moments is painful because the cancer did some really terrible things to Ramone, yet it never touched his spirit. I admit I felt robbed on our wedding day because I knew he didn't get to enjoy it. We were able to have our first dance on the dance floor of the reception hall in front of everyone but that was the only dancing Ramone was able to do. He began to feel so tired and ill that, half way into the reception, we left so that he could go home and lay down.

I remember feeling envious of everyone that attended my reception because of how much fun they were having. I stood sideline and watched all the laughter, dancing, and talking while Ramone and I were barely apart of it. I felt cheated by that cancer and I couldn't stand it. Of all the days it had to show its ugly head and cause problems, it had to pick today. Then I began feeling angry at myself for not marrying Ramone sooner. I had played many scenarios out in my head of us getting married and each one had a happier ending than what I was experiencing.

You see, within all the years we dated I never felt in a rush to marry him. We both just felt like, when it was meant to be, it would be, and left it at that. How could I know in the years prior that Ramone would have cancer, let alone feel this ill on our wedding day? Somehow as I stood on the sidelines of my reception, I became heartbroken as I thought "if we had only married sooner then he could've enjoyed our day ".

As we got in the car to go home, Ramone looked at me with sadness in his eyes as if he felt I was disappointed by him not feeling well. I wrapped both of my arms tightly around his fragile body to comfort and ensure him that, no matter what... I would always love him. As we embraced, I tightly closed my eyes and released a loud sigh as I tried to quiet the screaming cries of "why GOD?" My spirit desperately wanted to release. I literally choked back a faucet full of tears with constant swallows and just tried to rest in the moment of being in the arms of my husband.

Your word is your bond...
Especially to your patients

{Chapter 6}

He Kept His Promise;

Despite Ramone's doctors promising that we would immediately be sent to Maryland for his treatment after the wedding, it was 4 weeks later and we heard nothing. I kept calling Ramone's doctor making inquiries but his secretary kept telling me that she could only take a message and the doctor would call me back. Sadly, he never did and Ramone's health quickly began to decline as a result of him being off his regular doses of chemotherapy. See, Ramone abstaining from his regular treatment for a month was a part of the protocol to try the experimental cancer treatment in Maryland. So now, in addition to being off his chemo a month per Maryland's request, his physician's negligence added another month.

One afternoon, Ramone was lying on the floor very lethargic and wasn't he acting like himself. When I touched his hands I noticed his fingernails were blue. Instantly, I grabbed the cordless phone and called my mom screaming and crying asking her what I should do. My mind panicked and I immediately thought the worse. All I could hear myself screaming into the phone to her was "He's dying, he's dying" and I couldn't calm myself down. She told me to call his doctor and they told me to call an ambulance and get him to the hospital. When the ambulance arrived, Ramone refused their assistance and they left because they couldn't take him against his will. His older sister was also over our house that day and was near eight months pregnant. She began screaming and crying at Ramone to go to the hospital and eventually he agreed. His body was so feeble and weak from the remarkably quick weight loss that we had to literally carry him outside and load him into the car.

How do you stand on the Word of God
when your legs of FAITH are Broken?

Brandy "BrandyWine" Rankins

When we arrived at the emergency room, Ramone starting having nose bleeds. This was unusual for him and we couldn't get it to stop bleeding. Finally, the doctor on call stuffed it with gauze pads somehow and got the bleeding under control.   Moments late, Ramone called me over to his bed and said softly in my ear "Baby, this cancer is getting the best of me. It's winning and I'm tired". I immediately stepped back from the bed and started rejecting his words. I put my hands on his shoulders, stared forcefully into his eyes, and told him that he had to fight this because I needed him. "Please don't you give up on me, you can beat this", my voice cracked. He just looked back at me restless and nodded his head, confirming it was time.

I suddenly ran into the bathroom and locked the door to the stall as I felt my body shaking hard prior to bursting into tears. I tried to make myself pray but I was too overwhelmed with emotion. I just cried and held myself around the shoulders as I took in the picture of his face and the words he spoke to me. "No, No, No", I shouted loudly, completely ignoring the women using the restroom. Ramone had said all kinds of things out of frustration about being ill in the past…but this was different. I knew he was trying to tell me it was time but I didn't want to hear it; him leave me? No, I just couldn't even imagine it.

At last, Ramone's head doctor came in the room with the rest of his team. He told us that the tumors Ramone had previously had now returned and they saw many new ones on the scans as well. "I thought you guys were going to send him to Maryland for the treatment ", I snapped. "We've been waiting for weeks to go and

How do you stand on the Word of God
when your legs of FAITH are Broken?

Brandy "BrandyWine" Rankins

get the treatment and you never called us", I went on. "Brandy, Ramone is very sick, the treatment wouldn't have done him any good", he said softly. "So why would you have him get off his regular treatment if you felt it would never help!" I exclaimed. "Brandy I know you are very upset and its evident you are in denial. Ramone is just very sick and it's out of our hands now. We are going to discharge him to hospice and send him to the palliative care floor", the doctor said. "We trusted you", I sobbed loudly as I began jumping up and down trying to quench the anxiety that was about to make me lose control. All in one, I felt nauseous, dizzy, and weak as I tried to ingest the word hospice. "All this time you allowed him to be off his medicine knowing the cancer could spread...you gave us hope and you never even planned...you weren't going to send him". My sentences became run-ons as I struggled to make sense of it all. "Now you just discharge us like you are not responsible. **YOU ARE responsible, you should be ashamed, ALL OF YOU! I HATE YOU, I HATE YOU ALL"**, I shouted at them repeatedly as they held their heads down and quietly exited the room.

Ramone was adamant in telling me to have all of his family, along with my mom, to come up to the hospital. I immediately called everyone he asked me to and told them of his request. When they all arrived, to ensure certain people were in attendance, he called out a few of their names as they stood over his bed. As he called out their names, you could tell there was just something different about him. It appeared as if he had a hard time seeing, but he was very clear in what he said.

How do you stand on the Word of God
when your legs of FAITH are Broken?

Brandy "BrandyWine" Rankins

"First of all, I want to thank you all for coming. I want to tell you all that I am broke and have no money, so don't go to the house looking for any because there is none there. Brandy and I used it all up on bills, eating, and being here at the hospital", he said. "If you go to the house anyway looking for money, you will be very disappointed.
Next, I just want to tell you that I love Brandy. She has always been here for me and I want you guys to treat her like family. Some of ya'll haven't; and you know who you are, but again she has always been here to love me and take care of me and I want her taken care of", he finished.

I had no idea why he said what he did, but the way he said it was like a warning, and his voice was very stern when he delivered the message. A few of his family members immediately spoke up saying they would take care of me and vowed to treat me like family. I was speechless after ingesting his words but I would come to know later that they were prophetic. I would also learn that those family members who were first to speak out in agreement to treat me "like family" were the first later to try and torment me.

He Kept His Promise;

That which I feared MOST had come

{Chapter Seven}

*How do you stand on the Word of God
when your legs of FAITH are Broken?*

Brandy "BrandyWine" Rankins

The day Ramone passed still remains extremely vivid to me. Scans revealed that by this point the cancer spread from his hip and infested itself all throughout his lungs. The doctors said the fact that he was able to breathe, was a miracle. They showed the scan to me and told me the white portion represented cancer. Well, the entire film was white. At this position I was operating in CRAZY FAITH so I took that to mean that the doctors had absolutely no control over what was going on and it was completely in God's hands. I just kept thinking and telling myself that, not only was God able, but He would do the impossible.

Some of his family members were really offended that I was operating in that type of faith. One of them called me out of the room one day and asked me why I was still holding on. "Why don't you just let him go, it's time for him to die. Is it money? Is that why you are holding on? If you need money for the funeral or what have you, then I will give you money but let him go! "He said. I know that was one of the moments that I knew I was saved because I had particular words I wanted to share with him, but I held my tongue. I couldn't believe he was talking to me like I was God or as if I was holding Ramone's life in my hands. Then I couldn't believe that he even thought to say anything about money. Huh? What Ramone and I shared was far beyond money and materialistic things. To even assume that I was praying hard for him to live and be completely healed had to with money just exceeded ignorance.

The cancer spreading throughout Ramone's lungs caused him to go into a carbon dioxide induced coma; exhaling the right amount of carbon dioxide but not inhaling in enough oxygen. Ramone slipped into this coma about two weeks prior to his passing. The toughest part of the coma was not being able to talk to him or hear his voice. So many times I needed his direction, advice, and assurance about the situation, but he was unable to talk. I needed to ask him what he wanted me to do if, God forbid, he passed away. But, most of all, I needed to know he was alright during his deep sleep. I would lie next to him and try to say in his ear all the things I wanted him to know about my love for him. I never felt as if I said enough though I would spend hours talking and rubbing his face.

On August 8, 1999, around 5pm, Ramone died. The nurse had removed his oxygen mask to suction his mouth and, when she had taken it off, this terrible feeling came over me. I instantly jumped out my chair (I was sitting across the room) and told her that he couldn't breathe without his oxygen while she suctioned him. She continued suctioning him and shortly after his eyes rolled up into his head. It's difficult to describe to you what I saw in those moments, but his face turned very black and had a painful appearance. I knew he was dying. The doctors came in the room and without delay I began screaming "he's gone!" They looked up to get my approval to initiate CPR and I know it was only God that gave me the strength and courage to signal no. It didn't make sense to me. Ramone wanted to be resuscitated and I fought their moral committee so hard for him to get it, however, in that moment, I let God have his way.

How do you stand on the Word of God
when your legs of FAITH are Broken?

Brandy "BrandyWine" Rankins

As I screamed and cried I walked out of the room into hallway holding myself. I began releasing groans and moans that I had never heard myself make before. Words can't describe the loss that I felt at that flash but it was beyond grief. I literally felt energy leave that hospital as I saw Ramone's face turn black as he took his very last breath. Even though I was too hysterical for my mom to really console me, I truly thank God that she was just there with me because I needed her so much. "Awww Baby" she said as she sat there holding and crying with me. I never knew what grief was until I witnessed Ramone's death. I had never felt so helpless in my life.

There was a special lobby they had on the Palliative care floor. It had a beautiful white grand piano in it and several sets of extremely comfortable furniture. Through the large windows you could see the beautiful clouds and red sky over looking the horizon of downtown Cleveland. It may sound weird but, days before he passed, I would concentrate on this sky and the clouds were spaced apart, making it appear open over that floor of the hospital; yet, moments after he died it was like the clouds closed their formation back together. It was as if God had opened the heavens, received Ramone's soul, and closed them after. I don't even think just for Ramone's soul; but probably all the souls he collected at that time. No, I've neither read anything like this happening in the scriptures, nor am I saying this has anything to do with God's Word; it was simply a nice peaceful thought that I had pass through my mind during that transition.

The enemy will try To assassinate your Character But be still and know That Jesus is Lord

{Chapter Eight}

*How do you stand on the Word of God
when your legs of FAITH are Broken?*

Brandy "BrandyWine" Rankins

After Ramone's death, I faced some extremely devastating tribulations. For instance, a month before he passed, we were visited by Make a Wish Foundation. The Make A Wish Foundation makes an effort to grant the wish of a child that has a terminal illness. Even though Ramone was twenty years old when he passed, he was diagnosed with cancer as a minor and was therefore eligible. Ramone really didn't have a wish to travel anywhere, maybe because of how poor he felt at that time from the illness. I'm not really sure but I know, instead of a vacation or large gift, his wish submission was for them to pay our bills for the duration of our lease. We had about a good four months left on our lease and our electric bill was enormously high due to him being on continuous oxygen.

The Make A Wish Foundation agreed to pay our rent and utilities until our lease expired. They had us fill out the necessary paperwork and, not even two weeks after Ramone's passing, I got a phone call from the rep I had been networking with saying that the paperwork was declined because she was supposed to submit it sooner. I couldn't understand how or why I would be penalized for this but I didn't have the energy to argue about it. I drew up a letter and submitted it to their corporate offices explaining what happened and how I didn't believe it was fair or ethical. They responded with an apology letter and a check for about $140.

As a matter of fact, let me go back some. After Ramone passed away, I immediately called his mother and she contacted the rest of their family. She came up to the hospital and I sat out in the hallway completely in shock while they were in the room grieving with him. Shortly after, she and some of his other family members left and I returned back into the room.

Ramone's mother's personality at that time is really hard to illustrate; specifically because it was the total opposite of my mother and I find it a struggle to tell you in truth what I endured without disrespecting her. I would never intentionally disrespect anyone's mother because I would never want anyone to disrespect mine. So, what I will tell you is that Ramone was very close to her and felt it was his duty to support his mother in any way that he could. I believe the main reason he chose to start selling drugs was because she depended on him financially. He expressed that he felt his mother's finances were his responsibility and, unfortunately, I never saw her not condone him doing it.

The area they lived in had a reputation for lots of fighting and occasional shooting. I think back then it was important for his mom to live up to that reputation. I say that because she was an extremely loud and very dramatic speaker that would be quick to say "Cause I'm Miss ___ and ___ and I'll set you straight in a minute", or "I'll cut you this way or that way and beyond." That was the clean version of her words, you fill in the blanks.

Whenever Ramone needed a surgery she would always call up to the hospital the day of the surgery and scream and holler that she knew nothing about it (when she really did). A few times they even held off from doing the surgery until she got there and she would come in the room just...scream, cry, holler, and it would be quite theatrical. It would really anger Ramone because he didn't know why she would do this; plus it would delay the surgery for an hour when he just wanted to get it over and done with. I don't know if she did this to be the center of attention or what but it was a lot to deal with.

His mother had a problem with me from the beginning. I'm not sure of what her fear was exactly but she was very defensive toward me. Even when he got diagnosed, she pulled me aside and said the doctors wanted to know if I was still going to date him since he had cancer and, if not, I could leave. I wasn't easily intimidated by her because I genuinely loved Ramone. No, I didn't totally know what his cancer diagnosis meant but I knew I would love him through it and face the impossible with him. I thank God for allowing me to do so.

Some of his other family members would tell me that she would say nasty things about me behind my back. She even went to the extreme of moving into one the apartment complexes that Ramone lived in. When she and her boyfriend (who didn't work) couldn't make rent, she came to Ramone asking him for money saying "You take care of Brandy so I know you gone take care of your Mommy". I thought it was terrible to put him in a situation like that but similar situations happened often, and many times Ramone and I would end up in an argument about it. She never really sat me down and explained any wrongdoing she may have felt I did toward her and I didn't try to question her about it. To this day, all I could ever really do is speculate the reasons for her actions. In the end, many of her actions hurt Ramone but he explained to me that he had forgiven her for all things.

*How do you stand on the Word of God
when your legs of FAITH are Broken?*

Brandy "BrandyWine" Rankins

Pay attention to the details of the storm... The chaos is only a distraction

{Chapter Nine}

How do you stand on the Word of God when your legs of FAITH are Broken?

Brandy "BrandyWine" Rankins

After he passed, some of Ramone's friends and my family stayed in the room with me to provide comfort. We noticed that his wedding band and a cross he wore around his neck that my oldest sister gave him was missing. Nobody from the hospital had come into the room or stated they needed to remove his personal items, so immediately we became alarmed. We called his mother and she said she took the ring and the necklace. Still to this day she hasn't returned it. "Since Brandy has been making all of the decisions about him up to this point, let her worry about burying him", she shouted in the phone to my sister who had called her. I was beyond speechless and I thank God I didn't have a nervous breakdown at that point. For many months prior to his death, his mother stated that she had paid for and made all the arrangements to bury him. However, after his death, we found out there were no burial arrangements in place; the shock felt overwhelming.

The hospital attendant recognized what was going on and was nice and compassionate enough to tell me to go home and get some rest. She assured me they would not only keep Ramone for the night but would keep him while I made whatever arrangements I needed to. She told me not to rush and was excellent in providing comfort.

The next day, one of Ramone's aunts called me. I had already spent most of the day calling around to funeral homes getting quotes for funeral costs, so when she called me I was only partially into the conversation because I already had so much to deal with. The phone call kind of sounded like "Blah, Blah *did you find a funeral home for Ramone?* Blah Blah Blah well *you might want to check into this one called* Blah blah blah". I said thank you and hung up. Well, clearly I missed **SOMETHING** because she immediately called right back and said ***"We already have his body and his funeral is on this day. If you don't want to miss it, you need to be there on that day".*** Even now I look back on it and know that it was the Holy Spirit that kept me from flipping right there. To simply say I was shocked doesn't capture the emotion I felt when I hung up that phone. I just began shouting and crying and my mother came running into the room to see what was wrong. I was already tired and grieving, and all I could think was "how much of this can I take?!" I was his legal Power of Attorney and I couldn't understand how the hospital would just release his body to his mom without informing me, I was devastated! Just recently I found out that, once you die, you no longer have a power of attorney, so I guess that's how they maneuvered without me.

Furthermore, I couldn't understand how they were going to have this funeral without me. You would think I deserted Ramone and mistreated him; or just did something terrible to deserve the treatment they gave, but I hadn't. We all have our short comings but I was a good wife to him and loved him dearly. Ramone and I had the type of relationship where it was OBVIOUS that we were in love. You just don't see a young wife at the hospital each and every time a man's admitted, sleeping in the chair, on the floor, and sometimes beside him in bed and not know that she loves him. Many of them didn't even spend a night there and I couldn't understand why they now wanted to punish me.

How do you stand on the Word of God
when your legs of FAITH are Broken?

Brandy "BrandyWine" Rankins

Even at his funeral they called in their Pastor. Ramone and I had our own Pastor and was a regular member at our church for crying out loud; surely this thing had gotten out of hand. My father invited his Pastor, who was asked to stand beside my Pastor and the Pastor his mom/family called in. So, there were three Pastors reading his eulogy. To make matters worse, his eulogy was completely wrong.   We got saved and baptized together at our church when he was 18. He had never accepted Christ prior to that, whereas it stated he confessed Christ at an early age. To me, this suggested it happened when he was a child. There was just so much incorrect information in there. Despite that, the most devastating thing of it all was the minute I got to the line that read:
"He met and married Brandi in 1999, there were no children born to this union".

This was the only thing said about me in the entire obituary and they even spelled my name wrong. *How humiliating!!!!* That was when I wanted to seriously hurt somebody and completely give up. I felt so cheated. I included a picture of the actual obituary on the next page so that you can see it for yourself. For many, it gave the impression that I met this poor man with cancer, married him the same year, and we had no kids. What about the four and a half year courtship we had. It didn't even identify me as one of the people that remained by his side during his illness and treatment. The lies were absolutely repugnant and I just couldn't understand how God was allowing me to be slandered in such a manner.

How do you stand on the Word of God
when your legs of FAITH are Broken?

Brandy "BrandyWine" Rankins

OBITUARY

On August 27, 1999 Ramone Dante Peterson was called to his eternal rest after a lengthy illness.

Ramone confessed his belief in Jesus Christ at an early age.

In June of this year 1999, Ramone met and married Brandi Poteat. There were no children born to this union.

*How do you stand on the Word of God
when your legs of FAITH are Broken?*

Brandy "BrandyWine" Rankins

He Kept His Promise;

What about the fact that we were high school sweethearts and shared many memories? When you love someone, you take care of them because you want to, not because you're looking for any rewards or recognitions. However, when you listen to someone tell a story in which you are one of the main characters, and they do not include you or tell it correctly, just to spite you, it's heartbreaking. Honestly, just when I thought my heart couldn't break from that situation anymore, it did.

Last, a few months after his passing, Ramone's family had a headstone placed at the cemetery. The headstone had the picture of him from the obituary along with the words "Ramone Peterson, loving son and brother". Wow!! Did they really leave out the fact that he was a husband? At first, I thought I just would get my own headstone created to say "loving husband" but I had to choose my battles with the enemy wisely. To me, it was absolutely terrible that many of his family members felt their actions were in honor of his memory, when in fact they were disrespecting it by ignoring one of the biggest parts of Ramone's life-**ME**. Did they ever stop to think, if he were here, what **he** would say about their actions? More so, did they even care? I know there were many nights that I played that scenario out in my mind and it always ended the same way...with Ramone furious.

*How do you stand on the Word of God
when your legs of FAITH are Broken?*

Brandy "BrandyWine" Rankins

How do you stand on the Word of God
when your legs of FAITH are Broken?

Brandy "BrandyWine" Rankins

He Kept His Promise;

How do you stand on the Word of God
when your legs of FAITH are Broken?

Brandy "BrandyWine" Rankins

He Kept His Promise;

What the devil meant for evil, God meant for GOOD

{Chapter Ten}

*How do you stand on the Word of God
when your legs of FAITH are Broken?*

Brandy "BrandyWine" Rankins

Ramone loved remodeling antique/classic cars. He would repaint them according to the latest paint and rim styles and show them off during the summer months. The last time Ramone went in the hospital, he asked a family member to put the car in her garage because we didn't have one in our townhouse complex. She gladly took it in but, when Ramone realized he wasn't coming out of the hospital, he sent me to get it and she brought opposition. One of the tires caught a flat so I made two attempts with a towing service to get it repaired. Unfortunately, they needed a flatbed to transfer it and by the second attempt it was unavailable. By the third time, Ramone had already passed away and, when I tried to go back with the flatbed, this relative told me the car was stolen. Another one of his relatives later told me the car wasn't stolen and was given to one of his cousins.

The bills became overwhelming because I wasn't working, so I had to go back and live with my mom temporarily. One of his family members would call and routinely check on me. At that time, I was so plagued with grief that I didn't think much about her calls or the fact that I was telling her my business. For instance, I shared with her my financial struggles and told her I would be moving back in with my mom momentarily; that was a big mistake.

A week later, my townhouse was broken into and only Ramone's things (appliances, speakers, amps) were stolen. I knew exactly who had done this and right away I began speaking death upon them. Of course I have repented since then and thank God that they didn't die; I couldn't have lived with that hanging over my head, it was an anger response.

How do you stand on the Word of God
when your legs of FAITH are Broken?

Brandy "BrandyWine" Rankins

Shortly after that, my home was broken into again by the same individuals. When I arrived at the house and opened the door, I was horrified as I walked in to find the entire townhouse covered in water. Above me, there was water running plainly through the ceiling onto the floor, adding to the two feet of water I was already standing in. The sound was that of an ocean and, as much as I would like it to be, this is no exaggeration. The water was saturating the inside of my walls and filling them up. There was a strange smell but I couldn't quite make it out. I couldn't figure out if it was bleach or ammonia.

The electricity was off so my sister pulled a lighter out from her pocket and lit it so we could see. Seconds later, she took off running upstairs and told me the water was coming from the bathroom. She said a line from the wall that ran to the sink was pulled apart. Instantaneously, she picked it up off the floor and connected it back into the sink; the water then ceased.

I was so paralyzed with surprise for awhile that I at first was unable to respond or go and confirm what she saw. When I was able to move, I panicked as I tried to make sense of it all. "Did a pipe burst?" I thought. "Surely no one broke in", my mind second guessed. Clumsily, I stumbled as I tried to run into the kitchen hoping it would be intact.

The stove settings in the kitchen were all turned up to high. This revealed it was tampered with because I didn't leave the stove that way, days earlier when I was last at the home. "Did you think my electric stove was gas?" I said to myself completely perplexed. After calling the police, I ran next door to the neighbors that lived beside me in the complex. Many were home and, despite my thorough interrogations, I repeatedly stood dumbfounded as I heard the same response; they saw nothing.

I returned to the townhouse and finally raced upstairs to see if anything had been vandalized there; my heart sank as I slowly pushed open my bedroom door. The doors and drawers to the chest were flung open and rambled through, as it now stood almost in the middle of my room, completely away from the crawlspace against the wall it usually covered. The crawlspace was where Ramone kept drugs, back when he sold them, money, important papers, and anything valuable. Of course Ramone and I knew of the selected few who he trusted enough to let know this.

The police and fire department had now arrived on scene. They looked around and immediately started interrogating me. As the extremely rude policeman took my name and information, the firemen pulled out tools and began inspecting. I became tremendously frustrated as I tried to explain to the officer that this was not just a random break-in.

Prior to Ramone passing, he and someone very close to him had a disagreement. It was terrible because both Ramone and I did our best to help them when they needed it most. This person was a "hot head" and continually made poor decisions. They wanted to be a part of the in crowd and tried repeatedly to be recognized. We were sensitive to the problem they were having at home with their

*How do you stand on the Word of God
when your legs of FAITH are Broken?*

Brandy "BrandyWine" Rankins

parents and even allowed them to stay with us- another BIG MISTAKE! Ramone told me that, while this person was under our roof, they stole and lied about it, so things were never the same. I even had to intervene to keep Ramone from fighting him on one occasion, it was a big mess. During Ramone's last days he told me who he wanted to have his things. This person knew his name was not mentioned and became very distant and cold during that period.

"No, I don't think anyone broke in here ma'am, just looks like a pipe busted", the officer scoffed. *"You said the electricity is off and it takes both the gas and electricity to keep the heat on here. We've had some cold days, this is Cleveland after all, so I guarantee it busted, giving you all this water you see"*, he finished. *"Are you serious"*, I exclaimed. *"Somebody pulled out my drawers, pulled my chest out, and disconnected the plug to the back of the sink. Somebody broke in here and I know who!!"* I yelled.

A fireman walked in and explained how he had to shut off the gas from outside. He said there was enough gas in my townhouse to blow up the entire block. I was in disbelief. I pulled the fireman aside and asked him did he think a pipe bursting was the cause of all this water damage. He said no and, in addition to the plug in the bathroom that we re-connected, there was a busted pipe. However, the pipe was one that was inside the wall. He said that usually the pipes on the outside burst first from the cold. He further said the pipe didn't look like it busted from the cold but was broken by blunt force. In closing, he stated that, while he definitely thought

How do you stand on the Word of God when your legs of FAITH are Broken?

Brandy "BrandyWine" Rankins

this was a break-in, the police department would be the ones to make the final call.

It was no mystery that their final call would be a busted pipe. They said if I couldn't produce any evidence that someone I knew broke in, they couldn't bring charges against anyone. I couldn't believe this was happening to me. My chest tightened from the anxiety as I struggled to breathe. As I grabbed my head, my eyes flooded from the tears fighting their way down my face. That's when it hit and the terrible silence of the moment spoke to me. Immediately, I remembered what Ramone said that one night at the hospital. He gave me the list of people to call and he told them:

"Don't go to the house looking for money because there is none there. The little money we had Brandy and I have spent it up on bills and being here at the hospital. I also want ya'll to treat Brandy like family. She has always been here for me and I want ya'll to be there for her. Again, if ya'll go to the house looking for money, or anything else, you'll be disappointed because there is nothing there".

"Dear God", I called "How did he know?" I said. Did he have visions of their faces as they broke into our home looking to steal any money or item they deemed valuable? Could he feel the coldness of their hearts as they filled our home up with gas and stole his speakers? Did he know they were trying to hurt me? Were they so blinded by greed that they would search for something that wasn't there by any means necessary? How could they be so selfish to steal from me and never feel conviction that he didn't give them permission to have his things? I just wanted to ask them "How do you even sleep at night?" Did Ramone foresee our entire home filled with enough gas to blow up the entire block as me and my sister stood there with a lit lighter in hand, surrounded by it all? Surely, I should be dead...**BUT GOD BLOCKED IT!**

I realize that I will never understand whey they did all of those things. I do know who did it and I knew the moment I walked into my house and saw it in that condition. I want you to know I forgive you. For a long time after the break in, I hated you all in a major way; however, God and only God has released you and that hatred from my heart. I couldn't expect God to forgive me and my many sins if I didn't forgive you, and I made up in my mind long ago that no devil in hell would keep me from inheriting His Kingdom. I also pray that you will forgive me for anything I have ever said or done to offend you. My only intention was to love Ramone and be the best I could be to him; I know I was and have no regrets.

I'm sure people have chosen to remember Ramone in their own way. For some, it may have been a vision of him sitting behind the wheel of his ol skool car on a hot summer day; which made your mouth water from the orange candy paint it was dipped in and the racing stripes that hugged it. For others, it may have been something he last said to them, or how he was there for them when they needed him most. As for me, I chose to remember Ramone just as he appeared on the next page in this picture-A SOUL THAT RAN OVER WITH PROSPERITY, ONE OF MY BEST FRIENDS, AND, MOST OF ALL, A MAN WHO TRUSTED GOD ENOUGH TO SURRENDER HIS LIFE OVER TO HIM.

*How do you stand on the Word of God
when your legs of FAITH are Broken?*

Brandy "BrandyWine" Rankins

For years I wondered how I could properly pass on Ramone's legacy. Now, I believe it will be done in this book in a major way.

How do you stand on the Word of God
when your legs of FAITH are Broken?

Brandy "BrandyWine" Rankins

He Kept His Promise;

There is someone in the streets selling drugs right now that Ramone's story will minister to. There is a young person who has been diagnosed with a terminal illness and another that has become hopeless; this story will inspire you as well.

I can't say enough how vibrant Ramone was. Cancer didn't kill Ramone; he just simply had that cancer in his body at the time that he died. I uses to think he was too young to go at the age of 20, but who am I to say how old you should be when you inherit the Kingdom of Heaven?

God has allowed Ramone to bless me in ways that will last a lifetime. In his twenty years, he's touched people in ways he never could have imagined. Even through this book he will continue touching lives, and that alone is priceless. For a long time, I couldn't comprehend why all this had to happen to me. I know now that *"what the enemy meant for evil, God meant for good"* and that God has birthed so much good from a place that once harbored nothing but pain. Ramone, I pray you are pleased with the legacy of your life that I have painted for the world with my words. Beyond doubt, to be absent from the body is to be present with the Lord, and I know you are with the Lord. Your obituary said you were saved at a young age; however, when you accepted salvation at 18, God renewed your mind and your lifestyle reflected him. Enjoy Jesus' eternal rest and walk upon the beautiful streets which are paved in gold. My thoughts, love, and prayers always...
~Brandy

- 97 -

*How do you stand on the Word of God
when your legs of FAITH are Broken?*

Brandy "BrandyWine" Rankins

He Kept His Promise;

*How do you stand on the Word of God
when your legs of FAITH are Broken?*

Brandy "BrandyWine" Rankins

No matter what Happens or falls apart Around you... Keep holding on to God!

{Chapter Eleven}

How do you stand on the Word of God when your legs of FAITH are Broken?

Brandy "BrandyWine" Rankins

It was now three months since Ramone's passing and trying to find any financial assistance to help with my bills was near impossible. More than you can imagine, I became extremely depressed. As if all of the previous events hadn't been sufficient, the townhouse was in my father's name and there was over $4,000.00 worth of damage done from the water and break in. Sorry to say, I didn't have the money and, for credit reasons, my father had no other choice but to pay it.

I called community and county assistance programs. I even tried to apply for food stamps. No one had any compassion about my situation and deemed me to be an "able working body" as they turned me away. I really didn't want to go back home to my mom. I felt like I had come so far on my own and now it was all gone. Miserably, I believed I had failed. I felt ashamed and didn't know how to face anyone, especially since I began running from myself. I was angry at God for allowing all of these awful occurrences. I had tried hard to serve and keep the faith, so I didn't understand why he was punishing me. "Didn't he love me anymore", I thought.

Eventually, I had to move out everything I could salvage, which wasn't much after the water damage. I had to start over. I began drinking to help ease the pain but the pain was still there. That then led to me drinking almost every other day as I tried to escape the "reality" of my world. Many days I would wake up and feel guilty for simply being alive. "How could the heartbreak of Ramone's death not kill me", I would think. Depression is a powerful stronghold because I would also feel like I betrayed Ramone by still being alive and not joining him in death. My thoughts were severely unhealthy.

How do you stand on the Word of God
when your legs of FAITH are Broken?

Brandy "BrandyWine" Rankins

I was lonely at that time but I had completely shut God out, so I was surrounded by only darkness.

To add to the drinking, I started going back to the same clubs and bars I visited faithfully before becoming saved. I slept a lot. I tried to sleep the hours of the days away as a means to get through them. I wasn't eating so I lost a tremendous amount of weight and my hair fell out. Prematurely, I started dating and participating in sexual immorality. I wore numerous masks and developed countless insecurity.

No matter how much alcohol I drank, none of my problems were gone when the bottle became empty. It was the form of pain that consumed my entire mind and body. The different men I dated and/or slept with were supposed to hide it but I only found myself getting used, hurt, and entangled in soul ties. I lived in the clubs but many times a slow song would come on and the music alone would spark a memory of his voice, face, or smile and I would fall out crying. My friends and their boyfriends would carry me out the club as everyone stared at my uncontrollable grief filled behavior. This conduct became a routine for me and my friends. For the next several years, I would just exist and not live.

Even though I knew it was way too early to date, I was way too angry to care. The anger enveloped my mind. Before I knew it, I was even angry at Ramone for dying; and I know that sounds completely twisted, but I was. Then I went through a phase of wanting to be with someone because of my fear of being alone. I was afraid to go home to the silence that was constantly screaming

How do you stand on the Word of God
when your legs of FAITH are Broken?

Brandy "BrandyWine" Rankins

the reality of my loss. Back then, that was the only way I could process it all and I just ran from it anyway I could.

The first guy I dated after Ramone's death was Sean. Sean was a handsome guy; he stood 5'10", had curly hair, and was light skinned. Actually, he was extremely light skinned, more like high yellow. He had arrogance about himself that he thought made him fine. You see, he was bi-racial for his mom was Caucasian and his dad was African American; and unfortunately, there are many black people who think, the lighter they are, the more attractive they are. They think they have good hair and good everything else. Before I knew better, I was guilty of such ignorant thinking myself.

I dated Sean back when I was in high school, prior to meeting Ramone. He went to a school close by and we were both part of a social dance group. I dated him briefly while I was in the ninth grade so I felt that he was someone safe because we had history. I ran into Sean one night while I was out clubbing. We exchanged numbers and started dating from there. In the beginning, he would seem like a very intelligent, hard working man who had extraordinary goals in life. However, within a few months, I would come to find out that he smoked wet (**formaldehyde**-fluid used to embalm the deceased), and took ecstasy pills. The tire shop that "was supposed to be his job" in Cleveland Heights; where I often dropped him off, wasn't his job at all. The block that the tire shop sat on was where he sold drugs. It was entirely crazy because he would actually dress in work jumpsuits, and many times I would wait before I pulled off to watch him go inside the shop. It was all lies, lies, and more lies.

*How do you stand on the Word of God
when your legs of FAITH are Broken?*

Brandy "BrandyWine" Rankins

When I tried to step away and have nothing to do with him...he became obsessed. He started calling my cell phone excessively and, although I didn't answer his calls, he would flood my voicemail until it was full with his messages. He had been to my new apartment only twice and knew I stayed at my mom's most of the time. He knew that I was trying to adjust to living on my own since Ramone's passing and I never realized he was studying my schedule.

One afternoon while at work I received a phone call from Sean. Instead of calling my cell phone, he looked through the white pages and got the number to my job. Shocked to hear who the call was from when my supervisor announced it over the intercom, I was apprehensive as I took it. "Hello", I demanded! "Eh why you ain't come home last night?" Completely confused at his call and questioning, I said "Huh, what are you talking about? Who do you want", I sighed. "I know you ain't come home last night because I've been here all night", he snapped. "Whoa!! I know good and well you ain't at my house Sean", I screamed. Co-workers sitting around me immediately turned to my cubicle. "Whatever, I'll be here waiting on you until you get home", he laughed evilly. *CLICK* he hung up. I turned around and noticed everyone in the room was staring at me. I laughed nervously and turned back around to finish my work.

I went into the bathroom and called one of my friends and explained what happened. "Yeah, he got the right ones cause we been done went right on over there and got crazy with him", she snapped. "I don't care what pill he popping or what he been

How do you stand on the Word of God
when your legs of FAITH are Broken?

Brandy "BrandyWine" Rankins

smoking, naw he ain't crazy", she exclaimed. "After the kind of year I've been having, he ain't seen crazy", I added. She told me to pick her up when I got off and from there we proceeded to my house.

When I opened the door, Sean was sitting on my couch in his boxers drinking a beer and smoking a black and mild. He just smiled and looked at us both through the blood shot eyes which told us he was extremely high. He said he took my window off the hinges and let himself in. I didn't say a word. I calmly walked into my bedroom and politely grabbed my crowbar. Not sure which one it was; but between the terrible words I was screaming and swinging the crowbar at him, he ran out of my house, boxers and all. Clearly, I could see this man was totally out of his mind, yet I wasn't afraid or intimidated. After everything I had endured, all I could feel was rage. Actually, if I was scared of anything, it was the fact that I could've split his head open with the crowbar because that's what I was swinging at.

Things after that with him grew worse. It was crazy because I still dated him. I was at an all time low and I knew it. I was clearly off my rocker too! At least the drugs explained his behavior. I wasn't using anything; what was my excuse? Shortly after that incident, he stole my car and went to a club downtown in a place called the flats. I called up my same friend, who by the way never got tired of going on these missions with me, and she drove me to the club where he was. We had to stand in a long line and pay $10 admission. It wasn't long before I spotted him at the bar buying another female a drink. As soon as I made it over to him, I demanded my keys and he refused while laughing. He was sitting

How do you stand on the Word of God
when your legs of FAITH are Broken?

Brandy "BrandyWine" Rankins

on a bar stool and, without even thinking twice, I swung as hard as I could, connected my fist to his face, and knocked him on the floor. My friend didn't waste any time jumping in and expressing her frustration either. I definitely thank God because obviously he was a lot stronger than the both of us combined and could've hurt us. However, we jumped him and it was embarrassingly funny to the crowd that watched and laughed hysterically as we got the best of him.

Amazingly, it didn't stop there. He had girls calling playing on my phone all hours of the night; his phone calls were more excessive, and regret doesn't even describe what I felt for getting involved with him. Eventually, he went to jail, I moved to another apartment, and we completely lost touch.

I ran into Sean several years later while I was out one night and there was nothing about him that looked the same. Because his skin was so light, there was no camouflaging the big dark black circles under his eyes, or the near closed blood shot eyes he wore. His lips that were once a healthy peach were now charcoal colored and severely chaffed. His skin was coarse, his hair was long and uncombed, and as he was escorted by a woman who looked just like he did. There was no question they were both high off something. I remember being told that who you date is a reflection of how you are feeling about yourself. And as I deeply ingested his appearance, I couldn't help but thank God that I no longer felt so low. That was five years ago and I haven't run into him since.

How do you stand on the Word of God when your legs of FAITH are Broken?

Brandy "BrandyWine" Rankins

He Kept His Promise;

How do you stand on the Word of God
when your legs of FAITH are Broken?

Brandy "BrandyWine" Rankins

He Kept His Promise;

He's a GOD of second chances... I'm a witness His mercy endures forever

{Chapter Twelve}

How do you stand on the Word of God when your legs of FAITH are Broken?

Brandy "BrandyWine" Rankins

It wasn't long before I became used, abused, and beaten up by the world, so I re-dedicated my life back to Jesus around the spring of 2001. It was God's grace alone that allowed me to return to Him. I still didn't have all the answers to the questions I asked most, but I knew I couldn't continue living my life like that. I got tired of running and living a lie. I knew it was time for a change.

After a few visits with my friend to her church, I decided to join. The Pastor was young, about age 30, and many at his old church didn't like his non-traditional way of winning of souls. They locked him out of the church and instead of him fighting them about it, he started his own church. I'm so glad that he did because truly he is an anointed and powerful man of God. Since he didn't immediately have a building of his own, we temporarily used a nearby high school auditorium for worship. When I joined the church, we had less than a hundred members, yet it was a life changing worship experience. Today, not only is this Pastor's church located in one of the biggest sanctuaries in Cleveland but he has a daily television broadcast along with hundreds of thousands of members. Isn't it amazing where God will take you when you step out on total Faith in Him?

Before I went to that church, I had never experienced such raw preaching like that of this Pastor. After I joined, I didn't change all at once. I was still living on the fence, for I still went to clubs, drank, cursed, and so on. With all of that, when I walked into that sanctuary on Sunday morning, it was like the Pastor knew my sinful lifestyle and his sermons exposed me completely.

*How do you stand on the Word of God
when your legs of FAITH are Broken?*

Brandy "BrandyWine" Rankins

He Kept His Promise;

Here it was I was just kicking it at the club with my friends the night before and what was today's sermon about? Yep, you've guessed it, *being at the club the night before and coming to church the next day.*

"You can't serve two masters for you will love one and hate the other", the Pastor shouted from the pulpit as he began to preach. *"God says in Revelations 3:15-16 I know your works, that you are neither cold nor hot. I could wish you were cold or hot. So then, because you are lukewarm and neither cold nor hot, I will vomit you out of my mouth",* he finished. He was looking right in my direction so I instantly began rocking nervously in my seat with my arms folded and head down as I felt completely uncovered. *"How did he know",* I whispered aloud to my friends who were just as guilty as me. *"I know right",* one exclaimed as another shrugged and the last giggled.

At first, when the Pastor made the altar call I would ball my fists up, biting back tears and resisting the urge to go. I wanted to cry and release all the pain that was bottled up but I didn't know how. Many times I would feel a loud scream in my spirit that would almost suffocate the fight I put up to keep it inside. I just didn't know how to go back to God after turning my back on him. It couldn't really have been as simple as going down there to the altar. Sometimes, pride kept me from going; I would look around at everyone and wonder what they would think if I fell apart down there.

*How do you stand on the Word of God
when your legs of FAITH are Broken?*

Brandy "BrandyWine" Rankins

The issues I was dealing with felt very personal with God and I didn't know how to deal with them in front of Pastor and the congregation. The devil would feed me a multitude of lies to keep me in my seat, and I listened. I felt hypocritical and ashamed, and I couldn't think of any reason why God would still want me. When I was in His presence, I felt more than unworthy. The more I attended church, the more exposed I felt.

There were other men that I was intimate with after I slept with Sean. I had become a totally different person than I was when Ramone was alive. I had thrown all of my morals out the window, completely losing focus of God. I would say things to comfort myself or justify my ways like "well, God knows my heart" or "Maybe I should just come back when I totally have myself together". Little did I know; I couldn't fix me. I couldn't get myself together and break the strongholds in my life, only God could do that.

Within a short time I began to pick up my Bible and read it. At first I struggled with understanding the King James Version so a friend bought me a New Living Bible. The more I read the Bible, the more I became on fire for Christ. I noticed that many things about me began to change over time. I was still living on the fence but I started to make a more conscious effort not to. I began to feel convicted when I ordered that drink at the bar, or would find myself saying "oh my bad" or "I'm sorry" when I cursed. I stopped going out at night half naked and showing all of my cleavage because my lifestyle was starting to be addressed in the pulpit. The Pastor would speak out about wearing tight jeans and revealing clothes;

this indicated to me that, as women, we do this to conceal our insecurities. He would also explain how it was a lack of confidence that made us attempt to get a man by using your body instead of our spirit. These very principles went totally against my mentality and how I was living, so in time they began to challenge me.

I was very familiar with buying the tightest fitting, nothing left to the imagination, and it wasn't enough cleavage unless you saw my bra kind of clothes that my closet was filled with. All I could envision was clothes covering my body from neck to feet, and that just wasn't me. If I may add, it also wasn't the latest style and was just outright "corny".

God's WORD was demanding me to be Godly and I knew nothing about it because I was so worldly. Nevertheless, one at a time, things began to manifest deep within me. Soon I would look in the mirror and see me. I began to see past the fly hairstyle, name brand clothing, and best body" title I won in my high school yearbook. What I seen now was brokenness. I saw the tears that I never learned to let run down my face and the warm hugs I yearned to have for comfort but never knew how to ask for. In my eyes, I witnessed the weariness from the nightmares that role played all I tried bury deep inside. Beyond the eyeliner and foundation I saw someone running. None of my friends could see it and, before this moment, neither could I; but God saw it all along. The entire time he knew my heart and the hurts I worked so hard to drown.

It was right there, out of that dark place, that I began to cry out to God another time. I stood in that mirror and tears began to flow.

*How do you stand on the Word of God
when your legs of FAITH are Broken?*

Brandy "BrandyWine" Rankins

He Kept His Promise;

It was like someone turned a faucet on and I didn't know how to turn it off. Screams began to battle out of me through loud wailing and, like obstructed pipes, I began to blow.

   After I collapsed on the floor, I sat there for a long time getting a release from my tears; snot, and all. I closed my eyes and, like a small child, I just let my Lord hold me while I marinated in His peace.

He Kept His Promise;

Eden;
the place of
A New
Beginning

{Chapter Thirteen}

*How do you stand on the Word of God
when your legs of FAITH are Broken?*

Brandy "BrandyWine" Rankins

He Kept His Promise;

In June of 2004, I started a new job for a property preservation company as an account manager. There, I met a man named Thomas Rankins Jr. He was very forthcoming and gorgeous. There was just something about his spirit that I am still unable to fully explain. Have you ever had someone smile at and it causes an excitement that penetrates the very core of your soul? Well, that's exactly how I began to feel each time I saw Thomas. Undoubtedly, there would be an entire room filled with other employees but all I would see was him.

Our first connection was that we both were writers. He wrote both music and poetry, and I loved poetry. I was a performance poet and it seemed like every weekend I was going somewhere to perform a poem I wrote on stage. In fact, the week that Thomas and I had our first real conversation, I had just returned from a poetry slam in Buffalo, NY. After hearing around that he wrote poetry, I couldn't wait to use it as an excuse to strike up a conversation with him about it.

Every morning after punching in, we both went to the cafeteria for coffee and tea. The cafeteria was everybody's morning spot after punching in. "*Hey, how you doin*", I said to him politely. "*I'm good, how are you*", he said warmly. I sighed "*good, just tired. I had a poetry slam this weekend in Buffalo that I'm coming back from*", I said nonchalantly so that it wouldn't seem obvious I was trying to make conversation. "*Really, you a poet?*" he asked. "*Yeah, I have been performing for the past 2 years*", I said. I smacked my teeth, smiled, and sarcastically said "*what you know*

How do you stand on the Word of God
when your legs of FAITH are Broken?

Brandy "BrandyWine" Rankins

about poetry".   After that, we started to talk about different topics everyday.

The more we talked, the more I really enjoyed talking to Thomas. Although he was exceptionally attractive and I enjoyed flirting with him, I initially had no plans to date him. He was in a relationship and they just had a son a few months prior in March. I was in an "on and off again" ungodly relationship with another employee there who was Thomas' manager, named Mari. Mari and I met each other at a previous job we both worked at. Mari and I started seeing each other when I was around seven months pregnant; and he was not only a junior deacon at his church but...he was married. I can't even tell you how I got myself into that situation but I can tell you it was ten times harder getting out. What's worse is that, when Mari got the new job at the property preservation where Thomas worked, he got me in. See Mari was hired on there as a manager, Thomas' manager at that; and so he used his pull to bring me on board.

As much as we tried to keep it a secret, everyone knew Mari and I were messing around. He was actually the one who told me that Thomas wrote poetry. *"For real though stay away from him"*, he said. *"Why you say that?"* I asked. *"Cause man he into that writing and poetry and seem to be real friendly with the ladies...naw, nope, don't even do it"*, he warned. At first, I thought nothing of it but I did keep the poetry part in the back of my head.

Within a short time, Thomas and I began emailing each other at work. Soon, we talked about everything. I would tell him about

*How do you stand on the Word of God
when your legs of FAITH are Broken?*

Brandy "BrandyWine" Rankins

things going on in the ungodly relationship that I was in and sometimes he would give me advice. In return, he would tell me about his relationship with his girlfriend who cheated on him several times; however, he felt he needed to be with her for their son. Many times, I didn't know how to give him advice. After all, Jah'Mir was about to be a year old, LC lived in New York and was barely around, so I was adjusting to being a single parent. I never believed in staying in a relationship only to make the kids happy. Before my parents divorced, it was completely miserable living in a household with so much tension and arguing from trying to stick it out for our sakes. When they separated, there was a peace in the house that I had never known so, for Thomas, all I could do was listen. Telling him that I didn't agree with what he was doing on behalf of his son was something I knew he couldn't accept and it wasn't my place to convince him otherwise.

By September of the same year, we were both at the breaking points of our relationships. Thomas came back from our lunch break drunk and hurt, saying that she cheated again and this time it was worse. There was a sports bar across the street from our job that everyone often went to for lunch. He went with one of his best friends and came back to work completely wasted. He wasn't stumbling or anything but you could definitely smell it, and I was nervous that one of the managers would find out and he would get fired.

On the other hand, Mari and I also had also just broken up. I had stopped being intimate with him for the last several months and told him we could only be friends until he left his marriage. It wasn't that I was trying to provoke him to depart his union, but he always told me how miserable he was in it and how he wanted to leave. Often, I called his bluff just to see if he really meant what he said.

Mari's wife was a diabetic and, according to him, she would purposely not take her medicine sometimes to spite him. He explained that this would sometimes cause her to have seizures and it would scare him and their baby utterly. He said he didn't know if she was trying to commit suicide or what but he was tired of it. He claimed that he slept on the couch and even sat on the phone in tears telling me how bad he wanted out. He always said that he couldn't wait for the whole situation to come to a head because he wanted to tell his wife to her face how much he cared about me. Well my friends, he definitely got his wish.

It was 6am and I was awakened by the phone ringing. "*Hello*", I said as I cleared my throat. "*Hello who is this?*" she said. "*No, who is this you called my house*", I demanded. "*Can you tell me how you know Mari*", she asked. "*Is this wife?! No, you ask him how he knows me*", I said after sucking my teeth hard and showing much attitude. She must've knew I was about to hang up the phone because she quickly said "*wait, don't hang up*". She paused and said "*can you please tell me how you know him and if something is going on or not*". Against my better judgment, I sighed and began spilling the beans...all of them. The entire time I was talking to her, I was expecting Mari to get on the phone and proclaim his profound love for me the way he always did to me, but... he didn't. In fact, as I talked to her the more I found out how much of a liar he really was.

- 117 -

How do you stand on the Word of God
when your legs of FAITH are Broken?

Brandy "BrandyWine" Rankins

That Negro did not sleep on the couch; and every other excuse he told that I was foolish enough to believe was a lie as well. Furthermore, when I arrived at work, he had the nerve to call my cell phone and tell me that he could no longer see or talk to me. *"What!"* I shouted, as I hid in the stall of the ladies' restroom to take the call. *"What happened to, if she found out, you would come clean, and you just love me so much Mari!"* I demanded. *"I love my wife and my family and I'm not leaving them"*, he said then **click** he hung up the phone. I wasn't living saved then, so I totally wanted to stab, slice, dice, and castrate him where he stood a hundred ways from yesterday! Apparently, his wife beat me to the punch because, when he returned to work days later, he had noticeable stab wounds everywhere.

You wouldn't believe he had the nerve to apologize and try to explain himself to me. I didn't want to hear it. The worst thing for me, I told him, was that I thought, more than anything, we were friends and I believed him; every word. I never considered he was just trying to be a dog. Of course I walked away from that relationship feeling super embarrassed and stupid; and I should have because I had no business messing with a married man-period! I was very hurt and tired of dealing with men and relationships altogether. "Maybe I'll become a nun" I suggested to myself *"it's not like I'm ever going to marry anyone again anyway"* I concluded.

After Ramone died, I never thought I would marry anyone else. I really believed that and would bite anyone's head off who even thought to suggest otherwise. Satan filled my head with many lies and I believed I could never have more than a fling with a man. *"Who's gonna want me?"* I thought. It seemed no one was able to accept the fact I was a widow. Guys would try to talk to me and, once they found out I was married before, they left; or if they stayed around during the holidays, which were the hardest for me, and saw me crying from missing Ramone, they would get upset. *"Why are you still crying about your ex-husband, ain't I enough for you?"* Then, I thought if I did remarry either they would die or I would die; and after the pain of Ramone's death... I just couldn't handle going through that again. I felt cursed, and for a long time the enemy had me convincing myself that I was. "How many women do you know that became a widow at 21?" I often said to my friends. When no one had an answer, that pretty much sealed the deal for me that I was damaged goods.

Because Thomas and I started to communicate more frequently and were building a pretty good rapport, I told him what happened with Mari. *"What!"* he typed over and over on his screen and I hear him over in his cubicle laughing. *"It's not funny"*, I typed while sucking my teeth loud from my cubicle. *"I knew something was going on with ya'll...I knew it. He's so corny"*, he typed. *"I'm pretty tore up myself about my baby momma cheating on me too. I know what always helps me...how about you let me take you out for a drink? We can talk more about it and it will help you feel better"*, he typed. I paused for several minutes and then I thought *"what the heck"* and I typed him a message saying *"I would love too."* After that, it was on and I did everything I could to get Mari out of my mind.

Our plans fell through for the night we planned to get together and go out. Thomas didn't explain why he had to cancel but he asked if he could stop by and drop something off. When he arrived, he was dressed so well and looking so good that I instantly had butterflies in my stomach. I became extremely nervous and hoped that it wouldn't make me goofy. I invited him in and we both sat down on the couch. We didn't talk long as he reiterated that he couldn't stay and, right before he walked out the door, he pulled this huge stuffed dog out of the back of his coat and gave it to me. He kissed me on the cheek and, just like that, he was gone. I stood in the doorway for a good five minutes grinning and waving goodbye. My behavior was so embarrassing I must say.

Meanwhile, we rescheduled our date for the following weekend and, by this point, we started calling each other on the phone. He told me that he broke up with his girlfriend and that he was sure they were over. I was shocked that he had broken up with her but I was absolutely proud of him for taking a stand for himself in their relationship. I had completely stopped talking to Mari and it just seemed like the perfect opportunity to mingle and get to know Thomas.

About a month had passed by and now Thomas and I were actively dating. We were seeing each other almost daily after work and on the weekends. I was still going to church and invited him to go with me. Thomas wasn't saved and had never been baptized or really knew much about Jesus. He drank, smoked marijuana, and hung out a lot in the clubs for he was apart of a rap group that had many concerts. I on the other hand had been baptized back

- 120 -

when Ramone was alive and, even though I had already re-dedicated my life back to Christ after turning away from him, I was still living on the fence.

It wasn't long before I totally lost myself with Thomas. Initially, I looked at him as someone to have fun with or briefly date but our relationship had evolved to us frequently being intimate and me wanting a serious relationship with him. I had cared a lot about him and, while I didn't want to build any false expectations for myself, I wanted us to become more involved. I was just about convinced that he felt the same way until I started piecing several things together.

For instance, his car was a lemon, but we never could ride in it anywhere. True enough, it broke down often and he kept it at his close friend James' house to be close to work, but c'mon I did ALL the driving when we went out. Then, we both lived alone and, although we took turns sleeping over each other's house, how was it that he was at my house saying he had to leave because his son was at his house waiting on him? At first, I thought he meant his son was outside his house waiting on him, but then he made a comment saying "dag, I gotta go cause my son has been there waiting on me for most of the morning". Huh? "*Waiting where?*" I questioned to myself. "Does she have a key or something", was my next assumption.

My thoughts about it were interrupted by a constant nagging telephone ring. "Hello", I finally answered. "I know you ain't messing with Thomas", Mari was screaming and hollering in the phone. "You

How do you stand on the Word of God
when your legs of FAITH are Broken?

Brandy "BrandyWine" Rankins

can't be serious. Call your wife", I responded. "You know I'm his supervisor and let me find out you messing with him, it ain't nothing to fire him and then lets see how fly your mouth is", he said with an attitude. After that, he did a lot of cursing, a lot of crying-yes crying, and then I hung right on up on him.

The next day of work was here and I couldn't punch in fast enough to confront Thomas about what was going on. Strangely, he didn't come in the cafeteria for his morning tea, so I think he already knew something was up. This only made me more upset as I now had to find a way to confront him without causing a scene. I logged into my computer and instantly began writing him an email that read something like:

Good Morning Thomas,
I really need to talk to you. I have been thinking a lot about us lately and some of the things you have been telling me about your ex don't make sense. For instance, yesterday when you said "your son" was at your house for most of the morning waiting on you...what did you mean? Did you mean waiting outside in the car for you to arrive or does your "ex girlfriend" have a key to your apartment? I know she can't possible have a key WHEN I HAVE BEEN SPENDING THE NIGHT!!!! RIGHT?!! More so, if you are not together anymore,

How do you stand on the Word of God when your legs of FAITH are Broken?

Brandy "BrandyWine" Rankins

WHY does she even have a key anyway?!!!! I know this must simply be a misunderstanding so please explain.

Thank you much and have a great day

Brandy

A few minutes passed by and, because Thomas sat a row behind me, I could hear him nervously begin to type. His reply was a request for me to meet him outside in about five minutes for our scheduled break to talk. I became instantly upset after I read his email response because he didn't deny it. Therefore, I pretty much knew what he was going to say and I tried to brace myself for it.

When we got outside, we walked down the parking lot and as he began to explain I stood there with my arms folded, neck popped, and face firm. He cleared his throat about five times and stuttered as he tried to explain himself. "Please just let me come by, that way we can sit down and talk about it in full", he pleaded. "Talk about what in full, either you are still messing with her or you are not", I snapped. "It's just that since we are at work we really can't sit down and talk. Please just let me come by after work so we can talk about it, okay", he said gently. "Alright, I'll see you after work", I said with a big groan.

- 123 -

He Kept His Promise;

At last, it was time to punch out for the day and I headed home to wait on Thomas. About an hour after I got settled in, I heard a knock at the door. Almost instantly, butterflies began to quiver my stomach as I role played the worst scenarios in my mind. I opened the door and invited him in. I studied his body language as he entered and noticed his prior nervousness was now sadness. I signaled for us to both sit down on the couch because I was on the edge of my seat in anticipation of what he was going to say.

He started off by saying originally he did break up with his ex girlfriend because he found out she cheated. He said she threatened to not allow him to see his son if he dated someone else and that he felt conflicted. He said, at first, he tried to fight her on it but within a short time he missed his son and gave in. He elaborated on their routine by saying usually on the weekends she would come over with the baby and they would spend the weekend over his house. After that, the more he talked, the more it sounded like mumbo jumbo and it became a challenge to stay focused on the conversation. You ever talked to someone and there is no sound but you can see their lips moving? That's what it turned into.

I did blink back just in time to hear him say how sorry he was for hurting me. He finished by saying I was such a beautiful, intelligent woman and that someone better was going to come along and swoop me off my feet. In my mind, that was my cue to get up and use everything I had to slap the taste out of his mouth. Instead, I just sat there completely astonished that I didn't see any of this coming. All I could think about was the time I spent with him

How do you stand on the Word of God
when your legs of FAITH are Broken?

Brandy "BrandyWine" Rankins

laughing, talking, and being intimate. My spirit became extremely heavy.

Right away, I got up and showed him to the door. As I watched him walk out, I felt it happening…my heart began to break and I tried hard not to let him see. Deep down inside, I had really hoped he would be the one to come and sweep me off of my feet and make it all better. *"Silly me",* I thought as I slammed the door and tried fighting against the tears that began falling from my face. *"How did I end up here again?"* I said in a loud frustrating voice as I growled and groaned. *"When will you get it through your head that no other man will ever love you",* I said to myself as I sat on my bed and sobbed. *"Ramone, why did you have to die and leave me",* I ranted. "When you died, I should've died because look at me, I can't do this without you!" I screamed. "My life was just fine the way it was and look at me now…just look at me now", I cried in anger as I beat my face repeatedly into a pillow. As I heard Thomas drive away, I just laid there in my pool of tears trying not to drown.

- 125 -

How do you stand on the Word of God
when your legs of FAITH are Broken?

Brandy "BrandyWine" Rankins

He Kept His Promise;

*How do you stand on the Word of God
when your legs of FAITH are Broken?*

Brandy "BrandyWine" Rankins

Sometimes God has placed a comma where you have placed a period

{Chapter Fourteen}

How do you stand on the Word of God when your legs of FAITH are Broken?

Brandy "BrandyWine" Rankins

Several days after Thomas and I stopped talking, I received a phone call at my job from his son's mother. Imagine the look on my face when a private call was sent to my extension and I answered assuming it was a customer, and it was her. I wasn't even speaking to Thomas, let alone trying to be on some drama with his son's mother, who by the way I later found out got my number from an ex friend of mine who was mad at me.

In short, the ex friend was someone I met there at the job. She dated one of Thomas' best friends and he was known to date other women while seeing her. He even made a pass at me with a corny line one day while I was at the water fountain. "Dag, I thought milk did a body good. I need to start drinkin some water so I can get a body like yours", he said smoothly. When I tried to tell her about it, she took his word over mine so I left it alone. He later tried to talk to one of my friends, which I had nothing to do with, and went out on one date with her. After things didn't work out, he decided to confess it to her; however, just for the fact that he said "Brandy's friend", she automatically assumed that I was involved. So, out of spite, she called Thomas' son's mother, who she was cool with, and told her all about me. To sum it all up, it was a hot mess and, not only was I unknowingly in the middle of it; baby mama was now calling my job.

"Thank you for calling, this is Brandy how may I help you", I answered. "Hello", she snapped. "How may I help you", I repeated. "Help me", she sarcastically responded. "Who would you like to speak to?" I questioned at that point thinking they had the wrong number. "I called you didn't I?" she said furiously. "This is Thomas'

*How do you stand on the Word of God
when your legs of FAITH are Broken?*

Brandy "BrandyWine" Rankins

girlfriend and you better stay away from him", she demanded. "What!" I snapped "You heard me, you don't me want to come up there and beat you down", she added. I laughed "Look, I don't know who you are or who done told you wrong but come on up here and watch you catch my fist in your..." I have to end it right there because unfortunately that conversation consisted of a lot of cursing, threats, and ultimately got out of control.

For the next several months, Thomas and I became an on again off again thing until things absolutely went haywire. Not only did we resort to sneaking around outside of work but we began sneaking around all about the job's premises also. The phone calls from his son's mother were now coming in several times a day and not just to my desk but to my cell phone too. She would call and threaten me and I would call her threatening her, it seemed like the cycle was endless. She said she was coming to my job to fight me so many times that I kept an extra pair of "fight clothes" at my desk.

It wasn't long before I realized I couldn't continue being the woman on the side; I had been there and done that so it was time to leave that type of foolishness alone. I was tired of the drama with his son's mother and tired of Thomas' having his cake and eating it too between the both of us. I told Thomas how I felt and we mutually agreed to leave each other alone. I think the separation many times was so hard because he was someone I worked with. I had to sit how I felt aside and put on a professional face daily to interact with him because we worked on the same team.

How do you stand on the Word of God when your legs of FAITH are Broken?

Brandy "BrandyWine" Rankins

We were separated for a few months, didn't see each other out of work, and no longer spoke on the phone. Our relationship had returned to being strictly platonic and I became completely okay with that. Speaking to him was no longer a difficult task and the butterflies in my stomach had died. His girlfriend would come to pick him up from work and I would turn my head the other way and keep it moving. I in turn began dating someone new and, in my mind, Thomas was totally a thing of the past.

Right before the year ended, I started receiving phone calls again from Thomas. They would be to ask me simple questions but they were still calls, and that made me raise a brow. Since I was dating someone, I always made sure I pumped it up to Thomas so that it would appear to be much more than it really was. When he would ask me what I was doing, I would say something like "Oh I'm just getting dressed to go out. My friend is taking me to an expensive restaurant" or things that he and I never did. I would sometimes put my hand over the phone to keep him from hearing me giggle in the background, or I would tell him about all the wonderful dates my new friend took me on. To top it off, I would thank him for telling me someone better would come along, because they did.

The evening of New Year's Eve, I received a phone call from Thomas. He surprised me with the news that he had gotten baptized a few weeks prior and was on his way to bring in the New Year at church. He spoke proudly of how he had given up smoking and surrendered his life over to Christ. I was totally stunned and speechless by his report. Thomas loved smoking and drinking so I just couldn't believe what I was hearing. I congratulated him and found it ironic that here I was standing there half dressed and on my way to the club and he was on his way to church. I felt so convicted from the many times I backslid that I could barely find the words to even converse with him. When I asked him what made him decide to get baptized, he responded by saying that my taking him to church with me many months ago influenced him. He said he saw the relationship that I had with God and wanted one for himself. I was absolutely baffled when I heard this. I couldn't believe that he gave up smoking, got baptized, and was now spending New Year's Eve at church! Before this point, I had never even brought in the year at church. It seemed like such a huge sacrifice and, while I wanted to in my heart, I just never did.

How was it that he appreciated the relationship I had with God more than I did? Or, how is it that he was now committing himself to the Lord in a way that I never had. I was definitely guilty of being one of those people that lived anyway I wanted but would be quick to say "I am Christian". The only time I had given up that lifestyle was back when Ramone and I got saved, but after he died I returned to it. Even after I re-committed myself to Christ, I still managed to hang around the same people, keep the same mindset, and backslide.

I knew I wanted God as the head of my life but I didn't know how to surrender it all over to him. I wasn't sure of how to put His will before my own or how to be disciplined against my desires. I knew my flesh was getting the best of me and I did not know how to stop it. Nevertheless, when we hung up the phone, he proceeded to church and I proceeded to the club.

To everything there is a season

{Chapter Fifteen}

*How do you stand on the Word of God
when your legs of FAITH are Broken?*

Brandy "BrandyWine" Rankins

As the year changed, so did many other things in both my professional and personal life. At the job, they were splitting all of the small teams into two large teams; placing me in a new department with new managers. I wasn't at all excited about this, especially because of the managers I got. I was no longer on the team with many of my current co-workers and it just seemed like too much to adjust to.

In my personal life, dating wasn't going as well as I had hoped. I really liked and enjoyed the guy I was seeing but he was more like a friend to me than a boyfriend. The more he brought me gifts or took me out, the more I felt this way about him. Don't get me wrong, he was handsome, humorous, witty, and extremely down to earth, but there was just no romantic chemistry between us; at least from my point of view there wasn't. I think at first I dated him because I was determined to move on from Thomas and all the drama that accompanied him. And while my focus completely turned away from Thomas, it wasn't fully on the guy I was now dating.

Thomas was still making phone calls to me here and there but there wasn't a whole lot of conversation between us. One night he text messaged me on my cell phone but I was sleeping. By the time I had awakened and saw the message, it had become late in the night. I responded back to his message and was very surprised to receive a quick response with a request to come over. I agreed though I couldn't imagine why he wanted to come over or what he wanted to discuss. One thing was for sure, I had to be certain I looked my best so I immediately jumped up and put on something nice along with one of my favorite body sprays. It was important to me to let him see that I was doing just fine without him.

When Thomas arrived, he had his son with him, and that alone screamed loud bells and whistles. You see, we never really brought either of our sons around each other. I was very keen on not allowing my son to be around Thomas much in the beginning because we weren't in a serious relationship. I felt it was senseless for my son to get connected to a man that wasn't going to be around. I also felt the same way about Thomas' son becoming connected with me. Our sons were extremely young at that time; my son was 17 months and his son was 10 months.

When we sat down to talk, Thomas explained to me that he and his girlfriend had broken up and, no matter how much he tried to move on from me...he couldn't. We spent the rest of the night sharing how we felt about each other and creating different scenarios on how to form a fresh start. Ultimately, I told him that I was tired of us trying to do things our way because it only brought drama and made things worse. I also said that, if we were going to try this again, it had to be the right way, with God as the head. He agreed and over the next few months we dated each other in an entirely different manner. We began to go back and forth between each other's church on Sundays, learned to pray together and for one another; and we really spent time just getting to know each other without physical intimacy.

Of all the years following Ramone's death this, was the first that I did this. It seemed that I had fallen into this cycle where I didn't want to be lonely so I met someone, slept with them, and tried to be in a committed relationship with them yet it never worked out. In the end, I felt more empty and lonely than I did before I hooked up with them. Then, I learned when I re-dedicated my life to Christ that I was developing unhealthy soul ties with every man I slept with.

Over the next several months I began to care about and enjoy my relationship with Thomas in a completely different way. It wasn't long before we both decided to stop drinking, clubbing, and completely live our lives for Christ. It was the best decision I have ever made in my life. Our friendship developed further as we attended church more. People began to speak into us saying that he was my husband and that I was his wife. And, while I knew I didn't have the gift of singleness, I didn't want to remarry. I believed if I remarried that I was betraying Ramone. So, while I grinned and bared the words people spoke into us, the idea of marriage completely terrified me.

At first, Thomas just laughed and smiled at these comments about marriage. I'm sure the thought of marriage probably scared the mess out of him too. Shortly after, God told me that Thomas was my husband. I know that may sound strange if you have never recognized God speaking to you, but he spoke to me loud and clear. One day I was following behind Thomas as he was heading up the stairs to his apartment; we were in the midst of a conversation and, when he looked back at me and smiled, that's when I heard God say it. I instantly frowned from fear and didn't know how to deal with what the Lord said.

He Kept His Promise;

Throughout the next few months, Thomas and I randomly touched the topic of marriage. After while I left my church, joined his, and we began to map out our future. We were thinking that we would get married within the next few years however, when we met with our Bishop about it, his thoughts were different. He explained to us that he didn't believe in long engagements and said if we really wanted to get married he would give us an eight month period to do it. "Wow!!" we both looked at each other laughing from the shock and amazement. We later made a decision to go forth and began marital counseling with our Bishop. I also took a grief recovery class at my old church because I knew that, before I remarried, I needed to deal with all my hurt and insecurities regarding Ramone.

In the midst of enjoying the wonderful news of Thomas and me getting married, I got a phone call from one of my friends. "*Did you hear about what happened to Mari's ex-wife*" (they divorced shortly after all that stuff with me), she asked tragically. "*Naw what happened*", I whispered in disbelief. "*She died yesterday. She was in a car accident down the way. She had a seizure behind the wheel of her car and hit a pole*", she said. "*Oh my God*", I responded. "*Oh no*", I continued feeling very guilty. I was able to locate Mari's phone number and I called to give him my condolences. "I just feel so guilty. I am so sorry about my part and what I did against your marriage. I would've never, ever wanted anything especially like this to happen to her", I said. "I know, and she didn't hold anything against you. It was me she blamed. In the end, we divorced and were able to amicably rotate back and forth with the kids", he continued. "Her death was nobody's fault, it just

- 137 -

*How do you stand on the Word of God
when your legs of FAITH are Broken?*

Brandy "BrandyWine" Rankins

happened", he said. I hung up the phone and none of that conversation made me feel any better. I called Thomas and told him everything that happened and he tried to comfort me in the midst of the guilt and shame I was feeling, but nothing helped. Nothing could take back the horrible mistake of adultery I committed and now this poor lady was dead. It was just awful and I felt so tainted and dirty for my past involvement.

Now of course, on the other hand, Thomas' ex-girlfriend wasn't completely out of the picture either. The fact alone that he had a son by her and was active in his son's life meant drama. She would still call with threats, except now they were mostly toward him and not allowing him to see his son. She tried to fulfill these threats several times, however, I encouraged him to go and get a court order for visitation. He did, and many times she tried to even block that. Too often we would have to call the police or go to some extreme to get him on the court ordered weekends that he was due visitation. She filed her taxes saying she was head of household, although they had already agreed prior that he could file this way, which in the end made Thomas owe close to $1000 to the government. "Brandy has a son, file him on your taxes", she said. One night she even tried to come to his house and fight him for becoming so serious with me and it resulted in her macing him, attempting to stab him with a kitchen knife, and her catching another case. She never hesitated to tell me during our arguments about the many times she went to jail or how "crazy" she was; I was never impressed. "You don't have nothing a good beat down won't cure", I always threatened back.

- 138 -

He Kept His Promise;

Many of Thomas' friends and family weren't excited about all the changes God made in his life. Thomas used to party a lot, so not drinking, smoking, or partying at all was extremely hard for them to ingest. They didn't know what came over Thomas but it was obvious that many of them didn't like it. A few of them even thought I changed him because I didn't meet them until after we surrendered our lives over. So they didn't see me when I was really out here in the world and, no matter how many times I testified to what I used to be, they didn't believe me. I think it's amazing that once you stop cursing, being quick to fight, and ultimately stop down right acting a fool, people will label you "corny". I guess I'd rather be labeled corny any day than go back to who I was before.

I faced conflict from some of my closest friends as well. Initially, I tried to still frequent the bars and clubs for my friends' birthday parties and just didn't drink anything. However, in time I found out that didn't workout either. Many times I found people trying to persuade or punk me into having a drink and/or do the things I used to and, when I didn't, they got angry. Because I valued my friendships, I found myself battling this for some time and continued trying to exist in both worlds. That's when I really began to understand what the Bible means when it says "you cannot serve two masters", and that you will end up hating one and loving the other. There was just no way could I serve the Lord and the world, even if it meant leaving my friends at that time behind in it. I loved my friends dearly but I loved and wanted to serve God more.

How do you stand on the Word of God
when your legs of FAITH are Broken?

Brandy "BrandyWine" Rankins

"It won't last girl, this is just a phase you're going through", some would say. "Quit bein a sucka and take dis to da head", another said while pushing a drink up to my nose. "She act like she can't come out and kick it wit us no more or sip something because she a Christian now, shoot I'm a Christian too", I often heard them quote. However, I remained focused on living my life for the Lord and, in time, many of those relationships faded away. Often, I would become sad about it because I missed my friends and we had journeyed "through thick and thin" with each other. I wanted them to come to the place God had me at, but life or salvation doesn't work that way. You have to want it for yourself, and that's the only way you can obtain it. I thought losing friendships was the peak of the storm I was to face but, little did I know, greater challenges for my character were approaching.

Shortly before I married Thomas, my mother was diagnosed with Lung Cancer. It was the most devastating news of I ever encountered; I felt so helpless and angry. It seemed just when I had found happiness, cancer showed its ugly head again, allowing history to repeat itself. Instantly, I thought back to Ramone's challenging journey with cancer and the huge loss I faced after. "Lord, please don't take my mom too", I prayed.

How do you stand on the Word of God
when your legs of FAITH are Broken?

Brandy "BrandyWine" Rankins

God loves me so much that He married me a second time

[Chapter Sixteen]

He Kept His Promise;

Thomas and I married on May 13, 2006. Our colors were ivory, rum, and sage. Lights and beautiful decorations filled the sanctuary and reception hall, compliments of Thomas' aunt Valerie. She did an exceptional job, especially on the reception hall; which looked like a white wonderland. Sister Shelly from our church personally decorated and provided a beautiful arch for us to stand under and, at the last minute, helped us to coordinate the wedding.

I had a matron of honor, maid of honor, eleven bridesmaids, and three flower girls. Thomas in turn had two best men and eleven groomsmen. We wrote love poems for one another and my friend Erica read mine as Thomas walked down the aisle and his close friend James read his as I walked down. He was escorted down the aisle by his mother and I was escorted by both my Mom and Dad. It was more romantic than I am able to describe and one of the most fulfilling moments of my life.

Moments after getting dressed and right before coming down the aisle, I was flooded with tears as I thought about where God had brought me from. Just the fact that he loved me enough to bless me with a husband for a second time was beyond any thanks that I could ever give him. Vividly, I began to hear the countless times I said I would never remarry and I just cried out to God as I now stood there as this beautiful princess ready to encounter the aisle a second time. I couldn't even believe how beautiful I was when I saw myself in the mirror. I saw a woman who had been through the worst but, because of God alone, still stood strong. I saw no masks, none of the same brokenness, and beyond the make-up was a real smile coming from me; a God fearing confident woman ready to receive her blessing.

Unfortunately, our day wasn't that simple and we were met with some extraordinary circumstances. For starters, Thomas' younger brother, who was also the best man, collapsed right after I came down the aisle. It was very scary because initially it didn't look like he simply fainted but began shaking a little, making me think it was a seizure. Thomas, my mother in law, and many others rushed to his side and moments later he came to. Thankfully, it wasn't a seizure and he said later that became weak while standing; possibly from the heat.

Subsequently, Thomas then became weak as a result of getting so worked up from seeing his younger brother pass out. I'm sure it really scared him to see his brother fall out shaking like that because it really scared me. I noticed Thomas began sweating really hard when our Bishop signaled us over to light the unity candles. I asked him if he was okay and, when he shook his head no, I didn't know what to do because it was the middle of our wedding ceremony. Seconds later, as we headed to the unity candle, Thomas began gagging and I just thought "OH NO, HE'S GOING TO THROW UP"…and he did. Now friends, he didn't just throw up because it looked like something out of the movies for his vomit projected all over the first row of guests. It was a hot mess, literally. All you could see was my mom, dad, and many others running from the vomit that shot like crazy in their direction.

How do you stand on the Word of God
when your legs of FAITH are Broken?

Brandy "BrandyWine" Rankins

Well, rewinding to when I asked Thomas' if he was okay; when he said no and I saw him gagging, my only reaction was to take my hand and help him cover his mouth. Oh, did I mention that I had on the pretty and expensive satin gloves that went to my elbow and matched my dress? Yep, those ivory gloves were never the same after that. And remember I told you that we were about to light the unity candle; we were standing over it when he began vomiting so, when I went to place my hand up to his mouth, I cocked my head down to the right and that allowed the candle to light my veil on fire. All I heard was my one of my friends screaming "Brandy, your veil!', and I immediately jumped back. The candle burned my veil quite a bit but I thank God that my entire head of hair didn't catch on fire like MJ at the coca-cola shoot.

Next, two of bridesmaids nearly collapsed. One before we took our vows and another when it was time to go to the reception. The one who nearly collapsed before the vows hadn't eaten anything at all that day. She was one of the people who always takes care of everyone else but neglects herself. That morning, I had invited all of my girls out to breakfast to ensure they all ate. While she didn't come out for breakfast, she arrived at the church with fruit before we dressed to ensure no one went hungry. What are the chances of that?

Next, the stretched hummer that our entire wedding party pitched in on to enjoy for pictures was a no show. When we called the company that we were renting from, they told us that it had broken down and they were sending another. Needless to say, another one did not show up and we didn't receive a phone call saying why;

so in the spirit of trying to keep things together, we put our game faces on and took most of our pictures in the Sanctuary and outside of the church.

As if you aren't already in disbelief, Thomas' oldest sister called and said that, right after she left the ceremony, she was in a car accident. I don't know all the details but, from what I do remember, somebody ran into her at a fast food restaurant right around the corner from the church. Thankfully, she and her son were fine, though her car incurred damages and needed a few band-aids.

In the weeks following the wedding, we received a call from our photographer, who is also one of our ministers. Now he has taken plenty of photos for us and his skill is unquestionable, that's why we asked him to be our photographer. He went on to tell us that, when he went to develop our pictures, most of the photos came out black. He said he couldn't understand why it happened and that many of the photos came out this way. Fortunately, there were a lot of pictures that weren't ruined and he was able to supply us with a nice amount.

When this chain of events onset, my Bishop immediately took us into prayer, for he knew the attacks were from the adversary. When everything was said and done, I would joke about it all with friends and family. I got used to the reactions I got when telling the story...all except for one. See, most people would respond "What!", "Oh my goodness that's terrible", or "You guys don't have any luck", but an Evangelist I know responded quite differently. When I was done telling her what happened, she said "*Oh okay so*

- 145 -

you have a kingdom marriage because the enemy did everything he could to stop that. Honey, you better stay on your knees praying for your husband because that's what's going to get ya'll through. There's something special that God has for the both of you and the enemy wants to destroy it, but don't let him", she stated with firm eyes and her hands on her hips. I received exactly what she told me and would come to know precisely what she meant.

He Kept His Promise;

The Anointing Costs

{Chapter Seventeen}

- 147 -

*How do you stand on the Word of God
when your legs of FAITH are Broken?*

Brandy "BrandyWine" Rankins

He Kept His Promise;

Thomas and I didn't waste anytime conceiving after we got married. We thought having one child together would bring our family full circle since we both already had a son by someone else. It was so exciting to be having a baby by my husband and a man I was greatly in love with.

I had a lot of morning sickness during that pregnancy but was able to continue working my job up until I went into labor. Several months prior to labor, I found out we were having a boy. I'm ashamed to say that, at first, I was extremely disappointed because I had always wanted a girl and Thomas and I already brought a son a piece to the table. My Mom used to always tell me that "God always gives you what you need and not always what you want". I found out for myself that she was absolutely right because, like all of my children, Braelyn brings a special joy to my soul.

My mom was going back and forth through treatments for the cancer and at one point was on strong doses of morphine for her pain. None of that kept me from being the brat that I was as her child because I selfishly told her "no matter what, I need you by my side when I go into labor." At one point, she was on a walker and I told her "walker and all, I need you." We both just laughed when I said it and she responded "I'll do my best Branny" (that's what she called me).

No matter what storms were going on in my life, having my mom around made the difference. She made the worst of things better with a simple smile, kiss, or "I love you". There wasn't much I couldn't share with her and we loved hanging out together. She

How do you stand on the Word of God
when your legs of FAITH are Broken?

Brandy "BrandyWine" Rankins

was the core of holidays and barbecues; I just couldn't believe she was sick... especially with a terminal disease. More so, I couldn't imagine life without her; I prayed and begged the Lord many days and nights that I wouldn't have to experience it.

The year 2007 went something like this for me:

In March, after successfully completing a second high-risk pregnancy which included 8 months of gestational hypertension (high blood pressure with pregnancy), I gave birth to Thomas and my first son together; Braelyn Thomas Rankins, a beautiful baby boy, and soon after we obtained custody of Thomas' son Toma'rez , who was 2 and a half at the time.

In June, my mentor and closest friend, my mother-Sharon Poteat, passed away with lung cancer, not even a year after being diagnosed. My Mother didn't have any life insurance so we had to raise the money to bury her. The funeral director told us that the cost would be $4600 and so I asked what type of payment plan options did they have...are we talking about a 12 month, 24 month, etc plan? He said he needed the money upfront before they could provide any services for my mom. One of my four siblings suggested that we may have to cremate her due to a lack of finances; however, I had no other choice but to believe God for the impossible. I put together a story about my mother that was entitled "Please help us bury our mother" and explained exactly what happened. Initially I felt embarrassed about

- 149 -

going throughout the neighborhood asking for money, but God said to me was I going to either allow him to meet my need or let pride stand in the way; I chose to allow God to meet my need. I gathered family and friends and we went throughout local neighborhoods posting these letters which also included an invitation to two carwashes. We washed cars, sold hot dogs, and did anything we could to raise the money; and needless to say that, within three days, not only did God give us the $4600 to bury my mother, but he gave us $4800. My Mom had a beautiful service and it was because of no one but God.

In July, my husband's grandfather, Thomas John Rankins, suddenly passed away days after having a birthday party. In August, I was fired from my job of 3 years when my newborn, Braelyn, was ill and quarantined from daycare for several days. All of my vacation and personal days were exhausted for the year, being that I took FMLA (Family Medical Leave) in March to have him, then took several days off to be with my mother when she first got transported to Hospice, make arrangements when she passed, and took a day off to support my husband at his grandfather's funeral during his loss as well. I faxed in all of the necessary paperwork from the daycare to my supervisor and took one day off, only to walk into work the next day and be fired without my years of service and extensive overtime taken into consideration. I was only told "We understand that you've had a tragic year but what happens if another one your family members die? We simply can't tolerate that here", and after 3 years of service, I was escorted with my things to the door.

The same day that I got fired, the bid to the loan on our first house was approved. All I could think was "Lord, how in the world are we going to pay for a house with only my husband's income now that I lost my job?" I distinctly remember my brother Jared telling me to trust God and that what God had for us was for us, so we went forth with the loan. On October 6th, my birthday, we received the keys to our very first home, only to find the police at it the next day because someone had broken in, stolen all of the copper plumbing/ piping, and did nearly $9,000 worth of vandalism. Several days later, we found out that we had a gas leak from the street to the house; that made the gas leak our responsibility and the repair quotes ranged from $800 - $1300, leaving us without heat for almost a month until we could pay the cost. Braelyn, my infant at the time, and I were both asthmatics and the cold air in our home triggered horrible congestion and bronchitis, which landed us in the Emergency Room. On October 23rd, the day before my husband's birthday, his mother was diagnosed with severe heart disease and failure. Her hearts ejection fraction was supposed to be operating at something like 55% and it was only operating at 5%. In November, I found out I was pregnant again and, in January 2008, we were on the local news because our mini van was stolen from church during morning service. To top all that off, co-workers from the job where I was fired were going around spreading rumors that

- 151 -

we were on television lying about the theft and that our van actually had been repossessed. (I guess the person who started this idiotic rumor didn't realize that my husband paid cash in full when he purchased it so we had no car note on the van for anyone to repossess it.) Can you believe the nerve of the enemy? I have seen for myself that he will stop at nothing to kill, steal, and destroy your destiny; but he is a liar!!!

Now remember I just told you in the ladder part of 2007, November to be exact, that I found out I was expecting again. Well if everything I just ran down to you above wasn't enough, I found out in the early part of 2008 during my 30th week of pregnancy, that my baby had extensive intestinal blockage. Only moments after telling us that we were having our first girl, we were told this diagnosis. The doctor also stated that our baby girl would need surgery immediately after she was born. This brings us full circle and back to the first chapter, where I told you I knew immediately something was wrong at my ultrasound appointment. I paid special attention to the way the doctor and ultra sound technician were standing outside of the examination room door grimacing and talking. As the doctor told us the news, I just felt something in my spirit break and instantly I started crying. Thomas placed his hands on my stomach, initiated prayer, and for several minutes we were just speechless.

I cried out "Lord, how could you let this happen to us...haven't I been through enough?" Once again, I felt deserted by God, but this time I had no choice but to trust him. I promised to never leave

How do you stand on the Word of God when your legs of FAITH are Broken?

Brandy "BrandyWine" Rankins

God again and I was going to honor that. "I don't understand", I managed to blurt out from my tears to the radiologist as he turned to the monitor and tried to explain. He said that on a normal ultrasound there should be no circles in the intestines of a baby. However, when he pointed to the area of our baby's intestines, there were so many large circles that I couldn't even count them all. He admitted that he was unsure if the blockage was coming from the baby's rectum or colon but that it was important for me to reach at least 36 weeks before giving birth. He recommended that we see both a specialist and surgeon and reiterated that she would need immediate surgery; I almost collapsed. I just couldn't imagine my tiny, precious baby being sliced on and I just needed God to turn this around. I understood what it meant to have "crazy faith" and petition God for a miracle but I didn't even have the energy. The enemy wasted no time to remind me of my past and started telling me *"See, I told you that you were cursed. Where is your God now"?*

After my husband and I left the appointment, we sat in the car for a few moments motionless and thunderstruck. Not one of us knew what to say to the other and heaviness began settling deeply into both of our spirits. The news we had received was totally unexpected so it caught us off guard. I had absolutely no clue that anything was wrong with the baby and began to blame myself for her being sick. After all, we were only expecting to find out the sex of our baby at a seemingly routine ultrasound appointment.

Subsequent to gathering ourselves, we drove to our close friends' Scott and RaShaun's house. Thomas and I have known them for only a few years but surely they have come through for us in ways that only people used by God could. Shaun is one of my best friends and is like a sister to me. I admire Shaun in so many ways and her faith and testimony alone is what drew me to her. She's always accepted me for who I am and, in the midst of any storm, she's always right there by my side. I will always be thankful to God for her. *"The devil is a liar with that report girl and we believe the report of the Lord"*, she exclaimed as she tightly grabbed my hand. *"Amen, we bind you in Jesus' name"*, Scott agreed firmly as he grabbed the oil and anointed everyone. Then we all joined hands, bowed our heads, and looked to the Lord in prayer.

*How do you stand on the Word of God
when your legs of FAITH are Broken?*

Brandy "BrandyWine" Rankins

He Kept His Promise;

"This will be your most challenging pregnancy yet!"

{Chapter Eighteen}

*How do you stand on the Word of God
when your legs of FAITH are Broken?*

Brandy "BrandyWine" Rankins

We left Scott and Shaun's house and went home. I spent most of the afternoon thinking about the baby and what the doctor had said. No matter how many times I replayed it in my mind; I still couldn't grasp the thought of a newborn who would receive surgery. I then remembered what a woman named Natasha prophesied to me back when I was only three months pregnant. She told me that this would be my most challenging pregnancy yet and that God was going to test me to see if I remembered where to go and get my help. When she first said it to me, it seemed to go in one ear and out the other, but it was now in this moment that her words returned to me.

I met Natasha through a mutual friend that brought her by my house one night. Natasha came in my house with a "hey" in her spirit as if she had already known me. We all sat down on my couch and Natasha began sharing all of these things with me that undeniably was from God. The Bible says that you will know if a prophecy is real because it will come to pass, and now it was coming to pass. I tried getting in touch with Natasha but was unable to find her phone number and had lost touch with our mutual friend. There were so many things I wanted to ask her that I didn't take seriously the first time. Most of all, I wanted to know if God was going to turn this thing around, and how. Yet, with each passing day I was learning that I could only get those answers from God himself.

By the end of the week, I had received a phone call from a specialist. She explained that, in addition to being a specialist, she would be the liaison between the surgeon, other specialists, and us.

She set up an appointment for us to meet with the surgeon who didn't have an opening for the next three weeks. "Great, how comforting" I thought sarcastically in my mind ". She further explained that the hospital my midwife would be handling the delivery at wasn't equipped to handle "high risk" situations like mine. So ultimately, I would deliver there but, immediately after birth, the baby would be transported to the main campus hospital, which was approximately a thirty minute drive away. "Another hospital", I quickly interjected. "Yeah, I'm afraid so but they're a really good hospital and will take extremely good care of your baby", she said softly as she attempted to reassure me. Last, she told me that the radiologist wanted to see me back for a repeat ultrasound at the beginning of my 33rd weeks, which was two weeks away. As I hung up the phone, I wept and prayed unto the Lord. "They want to take my baby away from me as soon as I have her", I said in a panic. "Lord, I'm trying real hard here but I don't think I can take this one", I opposed. I gathered my clothes, started the shower, and proceeded to get dressed.

When I got to church that Sunday, I told a few of the ministers who are also good friends of ours what was going on. One of them told me to anoint my stomach with oil nightly and continuously pray for the baby. I went down at the conclusion of service for prayer and the prayer that went forth over me was that, if it was His will, for God to reverse the report by the next ultrasound. "Do you believe Sister Brandy that God can do all things but fail", the minister asked? "Without faith, it is impossible to please Him, so you can't worry about what God did or didn't do in the past; this is an entirely new situation and you have to come to this altar believing God for

- 157 -

How do you stand on the Word of God
when your legs of FAITH are Broken?

Brandy "BrandyWine" Rankins

the impossible! You have to believe He will do just what you ask", she said nodding her head for my agreement. I nodded back and said "yes". Because of all the crying I had done during the prayer, I was offered some tissue by another altar worker. I wiped my face and went back to my seat.

I began to think about what the minister said to me. Here it was nine years later since Ramone's passing and one year since my mom's passing and I couldn't help but to recall begging the Lord not to take either one of them, but His will was different. The thing that frightened me most was that this would be the first baby I would deliver without my mother. I knew it was no one but God that allowed her to make it to Braelyn's birth because she went from being on a cane a few months prior to walking just fine and on no heavy meds. She even helped Thomas cut the cord. It was such a struggle to push Braelyn out. I remember the first thing my mom said to me once I pushed him out was "Brandy, that's enough, no more children. It's now time to get your degree sweetie". I always felt like I disappointed my mom because I didn't have my degree. I found myself many times wanting it more for her than I did for myself.

I didn't know how to approach this situation without thinking about what happened in the past. The truth is that I was disappointed with God when my mother died. I even stayed out of church for a few months after it happened. It seemed like, after her death, I couldn't hear the sermon; all I could hear was my thoughts toward God for letting it happen. I was angry and hurt, and I asked

How do you stand on the Word of God
when your legs of FAITH are Broken?

Brandy "BrandyWine" Rankins

"why" until I became blue in the face. (And I'm an African American woman so you know that was a long time.)

One day shortly after my mother went to be with the Lord, I was out shopping with my family. Thomas and I were taking all the children to a dollar movie theater and had some time to spare before the next show started. We went next door to a clothing store and were all spread out looking at different things. I was holding Braelyn, who was only like 4 ½-5 months then, and looking at some shirts. This lady out of no where came by me and said "Hey Grandma's baby, you know you grandma's baby too don't you", she said lovingly to Braelyn. "Say Mommy why you got me on these big boy clothes and you know my Granny said to let me take my time becoming a big boy", she said to him. Immediately, I struggled to fight back tears as my hands started to shake, remembering what my mom used to tell me. My mother would always tell me to take my time letting my kids grow up. With Jah'Mir, I never put him in bunny sleepers or anything with animals. I would put him in little sweaters and ties that I thought were adorable. Now I was doing the same thing with Braelyn. The big question was "how is it that this strange woman, who I never saw before, knew what my mom told me?"

"Ma'am", I managed to say without crying. My mom passed a few months ago in June and she used to tell me that all the time about my kids. "How did you know she use to tell me that", I asked sarcastically. "Aw sweetie, I am so sorry to hear that. I didn't know your mom but the Holy Spirit told me to come over here and say that to you", she said. "See, even from heaven Grandma knows

- 159 -

how to get a message to you", she finished. At first, I just stood there in total shock. I couldn't speak, I couldn't move, and I couldn't seem to put down the shirt in my hand that now lay clinched in my fingers. Then, that's when it happened...the tears began to fall uncontrollably and I was too frozen to wipe them or gain my composure. "Aw dear, don't you go crying on me", she said as she began wiping her tears. "Honey, I know what its like to lose someone you love and I'm right down the street at Lacy's Clothing Store if you ever need a mother or grandmother here, okay", she concluded. I tried to thank her but I couldn't move my lips to speak. Then, just like that, she floated away smiling and singing throughout the store.

A few moments later I managed to put the shirt back on the rack. I hugged Braelyn tightly and, as my face became lost in his neck I continued to cry. "Okay, we gotta pull it together and get out of here", I said to myself. I frantically walked throughout the store looking for Thomas to tell him about it but I couldn't find him anywhere. I pulled my cell phone from my purse and called his cell. "I'm parked in front of the store with the boys. I was just letting you take your time so come out whenever you are done okay", he said. "I'm coming right now", I responded as I found my way to the exit.

When I got in the car, I tried to tell Thomas all about what happened in the store but I couldn't get it out because of how emotional I was. At that time, I saw the woman leaving the store and I said "her right there bae, she said it." Thomas gave me a hug and kiss in hopes to comfort me. "What's wrong Mommy", both Jah'Mir and Toma'rez asked from the backseat when they saw my tears. "Nothing, Mommy's okay babies", I said. As Thomas parked the car, I wiped my tears, took a deep breath, and we went inside the theatre.

It was the day of my second ultrasound appointment and I did not want to go. My sister in law, Lisa, called me the night before to encourage me to go forth. I told her that I just wasn't prepared to see those circles if they were still there and that I rather just not go. "I know you don't want to, but you need to, and God is able. All is well", she said. Thomas and I got dressed, I pushed through the nervousness, and we went to the appointment.

Once we arrived, we immediately went into prayer. The receptionist called my name and we went back in to the ultrasound room. I was so anxious to know what the ultrasound was going to say. "Please let the blockage be gone Lord", I pleaded in my mind. It seemed like it took forever for the radiologist to put the gel on my stomach and start looking with his probe.

When the picture of baby appeared on the monitor, the doctor didn't need to say anything. There, loud and clear, were the countless circles and they were still very large. I tuned him out as he began to explain that the circles indicated the baby's intestines were still very much dilated. I could barely lift my eyes up to my husband, let alone God.

"Again, it's important that you carry this pregnancy out to about 36 to 37 weeks", the doctor said. "We need to make sure the lungs are fully developed and get as close to your due date as possible", he continued. "From here, you will have to meet with the surgeon and see what their plan is going to be", he ended. It felt so unfair and, once again, I felt like God wasn't there for me. I was throwing a pity party for myself and didn't even want to give birth. I didn't want to deal the reality that my baby was sick. I had prayed over my stomach hard; and I just knew when I walked in that office the monitor would give a different report, however, it didn't.

Thomas is an emotionally introverted person so it was so difficult to read him and his feelings at that moment. His face was extremely heavy with sadness and I knew I needed to be there for him, just as I needed him to be there for me.

He Kept His Promise;

Operating out of fear keeps you from operating out of perfect love

~Elder Jared Poteat

{Chapter Nineteen}

*How do you stand on the Word of God
when your legs of FAITH are Broken?*

Brandy "BrandyWine" Rankins

"OUCH!" I yelled as I was awakened at 6am by contractions. It was only days after my second ultrasound appointment and I began thinking "I cannot be in labor." I headed to the bathroom and was relieved to see there was no blood or other signs of preterm labor. I quietly walked down the stairs so that I wouldn't wake anyone up and went to the kitchen for water. I held my cup up to the faucet and, right as I brought the cup to my lips to for a drink, *"OOUCH"*, I panicked as the pain became stronger and less than five minutes apart from the last. I knew at that point I was in labor.

First, I tried waking Thomas. He sleeps ridiculously hard and the only sense I could make out of him was a few groans and some foreign mumbling. "Bae...Bae, I'm having contractions. I think I'm in labor", I said nervously as I shoved him in the back. "Grrrrrr", he grumbled before wiping the slob from his mouth and turning over in his sleep. The baby could be lying right beside him in the bed yelling its head off and he would still be peacefully asleep. I've witnessed that in the past with Braelyn, Jah'Mir, and Toma'rez; surely it wouldn't be different with this one. After realizing I wasn't going to successfully wake him up, I got out of the bed and went downstairs.

When I made it downstairs, I grabbed the phone, sat on the couch, and called my sister in law, Lisa. They were an hour behind where she lived so I didn't expect anyone to answer the phone that early in the morning. Lisa answered and all I could do was cry as I told her I thought I was in labor. *"Did you call the doctor"*, she grumbled. *"No, they said I need to get to 36 or 37 weeks before I delivered...I'm just not ready for this. What if she is sick or needs*

- 164 -

surgery? I can't do this without Shade" (my mom), I said. *"You gotta calm down, drink lots of water, and call your doctor",* she replied. *"Its okay, God got it. God got it all",* she finished. *"You're right, you're right",* I said as I tried to reassure myself before hanging up.

I continued to drink lots of water in hopes of postponing labor. The day before was June 6th and it marked the first year anniversary of my mom going to be with the Lord. I spent most of that day crying and grieving as I looked through pictures and thought of my mother, but I didn't think I threw myself into labor as a result of it. I had even planned my baby shower purposely for today, June 7th, so that I could celebrate after such a day of grief. My baby shower was scheduled for this afternoon and I was determined NOT to have this baby today and go forth with the shower.

I tried to lie back down but I was too uncomfortable to go back to sleep. I tried again to wake Thomas up and tell him about the contractions but he slept like a log. He moaned a few words at me, turned his head over, and continued to snore. The contractions kept coming but were no longer five minutes apart. I began to think that the water was working and I continued drinking even more.

Around 9am I called my doctor. I told her what was going on and she said that, while they definitely didn't want me to go into labor this early, if I did they wouldn't stop me. She told me to drink as much water as I could and elevate my feet. She said if the pains got so bad that I couldn't talk through them, to come in. I convinced

How do you stand on the Word of God when your legs of FAITH are Broken?

Brandy "BrandyWine" Rankins

myself that the contractions were going to stop and I was going to enjoy my baby shower.

I called Shaun and told her what all was happening too. "I still got a lot of…I paused for another contraction**OUCH**", I said. Then I continued "food to cook too", I finished. "Bran, you alright? Girl I gotta drop Isaiah off at his dad's and then I'll be right over", she said. Meanwhile, I hung up from Shaun and got started on the baked beans and barbecued meat balls.

A lot of people came by for the shower. It was a co-ed shower so both Thomas' friends and mine were there. Hours had passed by and we played games, talked, and served the food. We were just about to cut the cake when the pains got worse; unbearable to say the least. My sister Senequa saw me struggling and followed behind me up the stairs as I went to the bathroom.

When we got to the bathroom, I noticed some blood on the tissue after I used it. "Yeah, you need to go to the hospital", Senequa said. Instantly, I began to cry and said "I can't do this without Shade. What if the baby comes out sick, then what am I gonna do?" I sobbed. My sister grabbed my hand and explained that she knew I was scared but everything was going to be alright. She told me that she hadn't even planned on coming to the shower that day because she wasn't feeling well (she has Multiple Sclerosis). She further explained that she had a doctor's appointment of her own and had left me a message on my answering machine saying that she wasn't going to be able to attend today. She also explained that, shortly after she left the message, my mother came to her in a

How do you stand on the Word of God
when your legs of FAITH are Broken?

Brandy "BrandyWine" Rankins

vision and told her to get to me because I would need her. What she said didn't freak me out or seem weird at all. "That's Shade, always looking out for me", I said as I smiled and wiped my tears. I got myself together and told my sister that I was ready to go to the hospital.

You see, my mother not being there to go through the labor with me was one of the biggest reasons that I didn't want to have my baby. For one, I thought she would be disappointed with me for having another baby after she said to me "no more" right after having Braelyn. I didn't have my college degree yet and I just felt ashamed to be having another child and, worst of all, my mom wasn't here to tell me whether or not she approved. If she was mad or disappointed with me, she wasn't here to tell me that she was or to make up with me and forgive me. She wasn't here for me during this crisis the doctors were telling me was happening with my baby and , most of all, she wasn't here to tell me everything would be okay and that I'd get through it.

I had even talked about it with one of my minister friends who was at the shower a few hours earlier. She just took me outside and began to pray with me; it was only God that she knew just exactly what to say. She prayed that God would give me peace over the situation no matter how it turned out; and she prayed that I would just begin to feel my mother's love and be saturated with her presence during this time.

I told my husband and Shaun that I was ready to go to the hospital. We told everyone at the shower what was going on and

*How do you stand on the Word of God
when your legs of FAITH are Broken?*

Brandy "BrandyWine" Rankins

that we were sorry but we had to get to the hospital and possibly deliver the baby. Everyone was relieved to see me go because I was having contractions all throughout the shower and everyone knew I should've left sooner. My good friends Delecia, Shawana, and a few others began cleaning and putting up the food. I grabbed my big yellow envelope where I kept many photos of my mom. I knew my mom couldn't be there for the delivery but I found comfort in keeping her photos by my side for the journey.

The contractions were becoming unbearable. I sat down on the couch a few more times before finally loading into the car. Shaun's husband Scott grabbed the boys, Shaun got in the car with me and Thomas, and Senequa and my niece followed in her car behind; and we were off to the hospital.

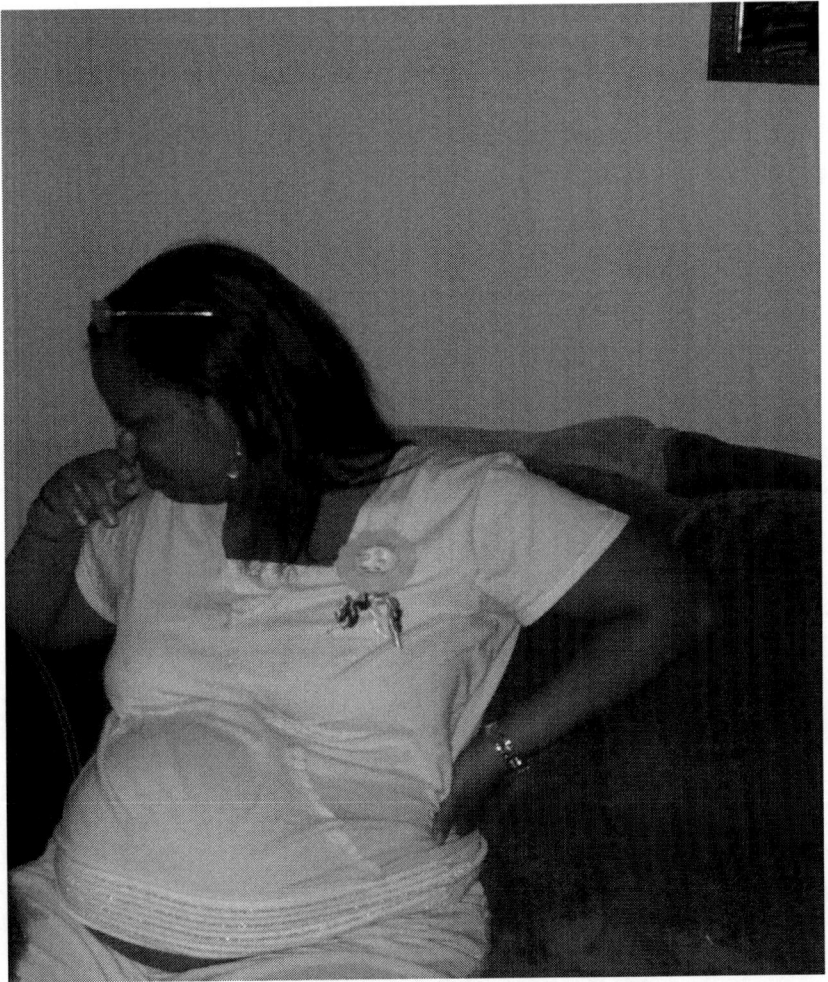

- 169 -

*How do you stand on the Word of God
when your legs of FAITH are Broken?*

Brandy "BrandyWine" Rankins

He Kept His Promise;

How do you stand on the Word of God
when your legs of FAITH are Broken?

Brandy "BrandyWine" Rankins

"If Jesus can get on the cross for us, Then surely you can get on the cross for your daughter.

~Lady Linda Lipford

{Chapter Twenty}

*How do you stand on the Word of God
when your legs of FAITH are Broken?*

Brandy "BrandyWine" Rankins

He Kept His Promise;

Lady Linda, the co-founder and former First Lady of my church, met me at the hospital. Lady Linda is a very dear and close friend of mine that I've had the pleasure of being blessed by for sometime now. Initially, I was drawn to her because of how much we had in common; for instance, we were both widows and we both lost our mothers to lung cancer. I had expressed to Lady Linda in my earlier months of pregnancy how I felt about having a baby without my mother; especially going through the labor process. "If you call me when you go into labor, no matter where I am or what I'm doing, I will be there...and that's a promise", she said. I'm sure she had no idea that her words really meant the world to me.

I was already registered on the Labor and Delivery floor so they got me a room and had me change into a gown. They paged my midwife, who was already on call, and had the house doctor assess me. I was dilated six and a half centimeters, and definitely moving fast in the labor progression. They would only allow two people in the room with me, so my sister Senequa and Lady Linda came back with Thomas and me while my friend Shaun sat in the waiting room. I was so upset that the nurses wouldn't let Shaun come on back there with me along with everyone else...I didn't want her to miss a thing!

My midwife arrived and told me that she wanted me to get an epidural to slow my dilating. She explained that there is a test for group B step that is done further along in the pregnancy and, since I hadn't yet been tested, she needed to treat me with antibiotics as a precaution. She said that the antibiotics were distributed twice over the course of a few hours with a break in between and, if I

How do you stand on the Word of God
when your legs of FAITH are Broken?

Brandy "BrandyWine" Rankins

continued dilating at the rate I was already going, she would be unable to treat me. Originally, I agreed to get the epidural; however, after meeting with the anesthesiologist, I changed my mind.

When the anesthesiologist came in and spoke with me, he went over all the side effects that can occur as a result of getting an epidural. I had an epidural in the past with both Jah'Mir and Braelyn so I knew the most important side effect of all, and that was being paralyzed if they hit the spine incorrectly. As the anesthesiologist began to explain the other side effects involved, I began to only see his lips moving, for I heard God say "trust me". I continued to hear God repeat "trust me" and so I turned the epidural down. This made my midwife almost ballistic and my sister upset. "See, that's why Mom needs to be here because she would've made you get that epidural", Senequa ranted. "Why did you explain all of those side effects to her in that way? Now you done probably scared her out of getting it and I need to slow her down", my midwife yelled at the anesthesiologist. Thomas just grabbed my hand as I sat there firm faced in my decision.

"Do you think I can go natural", I asked my nurse who was driving me crazy by continuously repositioning the monitor on my stomach to read the baby's heartbeat. "I definitely think you can but you can barely take the doctor's fingers when she checks to see how dilated you are. You are going to have to relax and press your bum down as she checks you. And stop fighting your contractions, and breathe through the pain so you can save your energy for when its time to push", she replied. Despite all the pain I

How do you stand on the Word of God
when your legs of FAITH are Broken?

Brandy "BrandyWine" Rankins

was in from the contractions, I took in what she said and immediately started practicing it.

When I dilated to nine centimeters, another specialist whose name I can't remember came into the room and said "Hi Mrs. Rankins! I've been involved with studying your chart and we believe that your baby doesn't have a rectum". Without delay, I started pleading the blood of Jesus and tuned her totally out. "The devil is a liar", I panted. She continued speaking only a few seconds longer before exiting the room. The midwife had manually broken my water once I reached eight centimeters and, by now, green fluid started gushing out with it. "Well, we know that your baby has a rectum", the midwife shouted with joy "because she just had a bowel movement". "Thank you Lord", I grunted in between the contractions. Then another doctor explained the baby was not supposed to have a bowel movement yet because it can cause aspiration pneumonia, its called meconium staining; so Thomas and I began pleading the blood of Jesus again.

When I hit ten centimeters, the pain had grown even more intense and I was literally screaming for the epidural. "It's too late for it now, that's why I tried to encourage you to get earlier on", my midwife scoffed sarcastically. The pain was so powerful by this point that it became almost impossible to listen to what my midwife was instructing me to do. For instance, she began telling me to lift my legs up and start pushing through the contractions. What I did instead was take the palm of my open hand and used it to beat myself in the head hysterically while talking myself through the pain. "I wish you were here Shade, I wish you were Shade" was all I kept thinking over and over again.

"C'mon Brandy you can do this", my midwife shouted while looking for the baby's head. "Her heart rate is dropping and we have to get her out of here now", she demanded. It was at that exact moment that I had the greatest de ja vu; you see when I was delivering Braelyn, my mother took one of the hospital's white wash cloths and used it as a cold compress on my face. I got so irritated by her doing this because she was wiping me so frantically that I could barely breathe. "Mom", I shouted. "Oh just hush it's making my nerves better", my mother said. I laugh every time that I remember it. Well how about my midwife, who by the way wasn't even the same one that delivered Braelyn, went and grabbed a white wash cloth. She ran cold water on it and I promise you she began wiping my face exactly the same way my mother did with Braelyn. Never have I felt my mother's spirit with me more than I did in that moment. Instantly, tears started pouring down my face. My midwife hit a button and immediately a team from the Neonatal Intensive Care Unit (NICU) came running in my room and breaking down medical tables.

Lady Linda came over to me, grabbed my hand tightly, and said:

"If Jesus can get on the cross for us,
then surely you can get on the cross for your daughter.
She's in trouble, now get past the pain and push her out!"

- 175 -

How do you stand on the Word of God
when your legs of FAITH are Broken?

Brandy "BrandyWine" Rankins

After the white wash cloth and Lady Linda's words, God gave me the strength I needed to push the baby out. It was the worst pain I have ever felt in my life, especially without an epidural, but God got me through it. "Now we are not going to stimulate her to cry because we don't know how intensive her complications are okay", my midwife said. "Okay", I acknowledged as I saw my baby come out without a sound. The doctors briefly checked the baby out inside the incubator parked across the room and removed the bowel from her mouth.

Months earlier, Thomas and I decided to name our daughter Brielle. I found the name and instantly fell in love with it when I saw that it meant **"God is my might"**. Furthermore, I loved it because it started with the letters Br, just like Brandy and Braelyn. As weak as I was and still having the shakes from the labor process, there was no greater joy than holding Brielle in my arms. I looked in her eyes and it took nothing for me to fall in love with her. She was still covered in a white substance, for they didn't clean her off yet, but she was so bright eyed and alert as she looked around the room. They rushed her off to the NICU and prepared me for a room in the postpartum unit.

I felt helpless as I sat there in a wheelchair watching Brielle plugged up to what seemed to be hundreds of tubes in the NICU. One tube ran from her mouth to her stomach and the doctors said they pulled off 25 ounces of stool from her stomach, which had backed up as a result of the blockage. The stool was being vacuumed into a large measuring canister. Her eyes were closed and her little body looked exhausted as she took rapid breaths.

Just as I felt myself begin to question God, I heard His voice say again *"trust me"*. *"We will be transporting her in an hour by ambulance to the main campus hospital"*, a nurse came by and said. It was in that moment that I was able to really appreciate sacrifice and could only imagine what Christ felt like on the cross. I mean, here I was in so much physical pain from having a baby with no medicine; and that pain couldn't touch the heartbreak I felt of knowing they were about to take her away. "Trust me", God's words continued to echo over my tears.

About an hour later, the paramedic team transporting Brielle to the main hospital brought her by my room before they left. Brielle was inside a portable incubator, which was made in the shape of a large rectangle with two circular doors on both sides. The doors are for your arms and hands so that you can touch the baby while they're inside. Brielle lay fast asleep from the exhausting journey of labor and the medicine they used to make her comfortable with all the tubes they had in place. She was swaddled in a bunny blanket with a pink and blue fuzzy hat to match. I had asked Thomas to go over with her to the hospital because I didn't want her to be there alone. I know that was hard for Thomas because he didn't want to leave me alone either; especially at a completely different hospital, but I insisted he go.

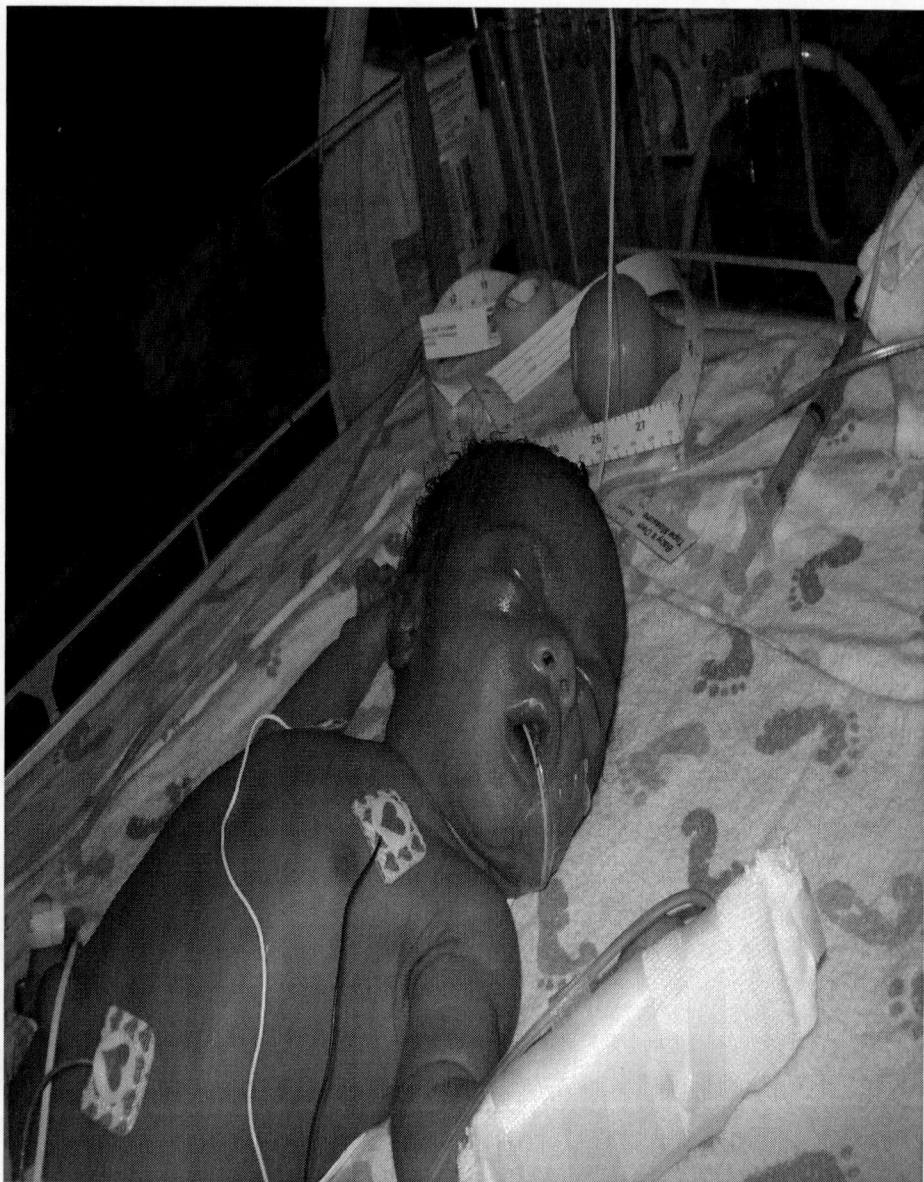

- 178 -

How do you stand on the Word of God
when your legs of FAITH are Broken?

Brandy "BrandyWine" Rankins

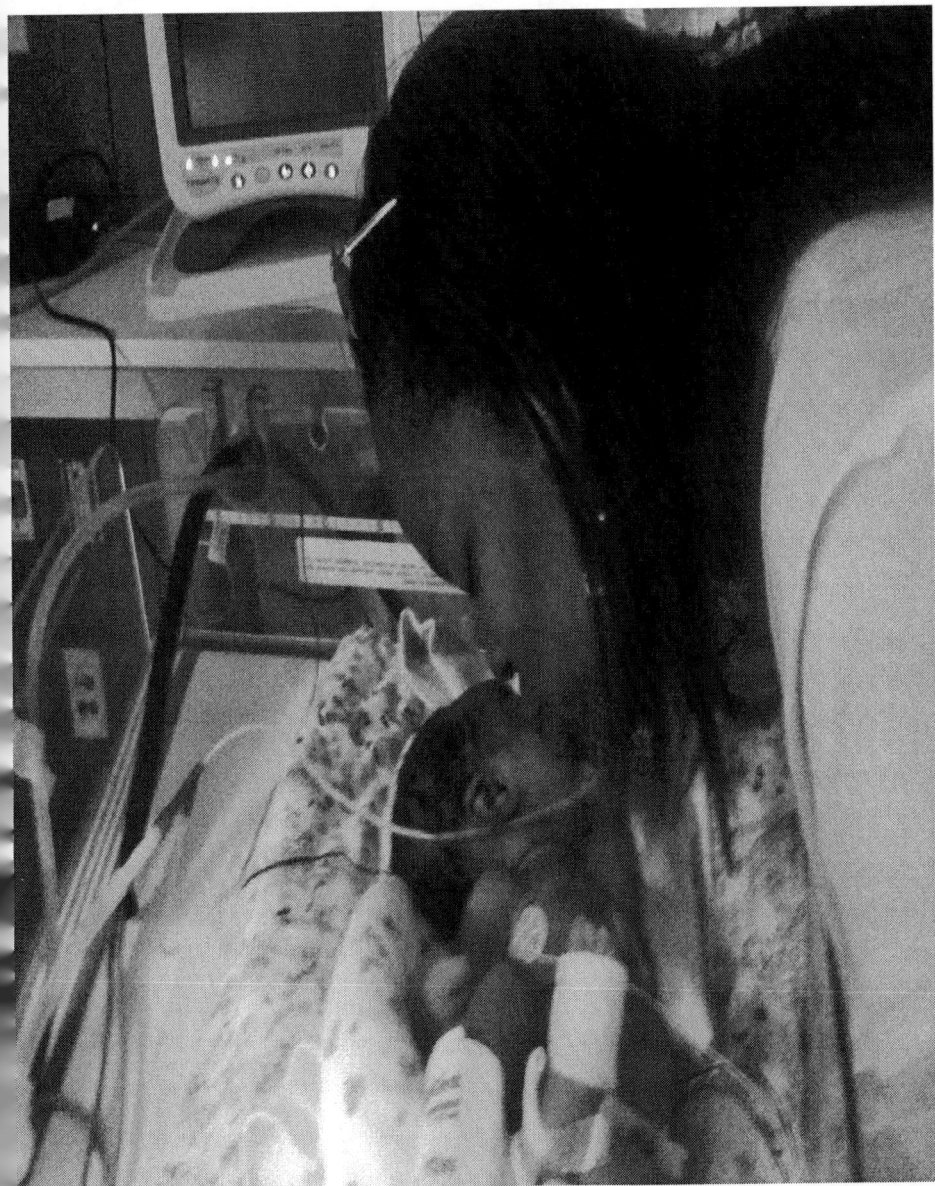

How do you stand on the Word of God
when your legs of FAITH are Broken?

Brandy "BrandyWine" Rankins

He Kept His Promise;

The moment had come for them to take Brielle away and it was heartbreaking to be separated from the baby I just had a few hours ago. I thought about her ride over to the hospital in the ambulance and how I should be there to protect her, but I had to trust God. I thought about her arriving to a new strange room and me not being there to calm her fears, hold her hand, or sing her soft songs; and I became engulfed with sadness. I slowly got up from my bed and began limping over to the incubator, for I was still in a great deal of pain. When I got there, I tried to take as many mental pictures of her that I could; to last me until I saw her again. I laid my hand on top of the incubator, closed my eyes tightly, and said a prayer.

Moments later, I watched the paramedics, Brielle, and Thomas start out of the room and into the hallway. As they left the hospital, I laid there watching from my bed feeling sad and helpless. With my other two children that I had given birth to, I was blessed enough to take them right home; I didn't even let them stay in the nursery long. However, here I was now watching my baby as she was being transferred to a completely different hospital and I couldn't even go with her. I couldn't hold her, comfort her, or even take her home. All I could do is push past my lack of understanding and trust God; which was the greatest thing within my power to do. I decided not to let the anxiety and fear I felt get the best of me. I pulled my cover up over me, readjusted myself on my pillow, turned over, and went to sleep.

How do you stand on the Word of God
when your legs of FAITH are Broken?

Brandy "BrandyWine" Rankins

The only way out Of the storm Is to "go through" It

{Chapter Twenty-One}

How do you stand on the Word of God
when your legs of FAITH are Broken?

Brandy "BrandyWine" Rankins

"Brandy...Brandy", I awakened to the doctor tapping me on my arm. Too deep into my sleep to be ashamed, I wiped the slob from my mouth and sharply sat up to see what was going on. I cleared my eyes to focus and was taken aback when I looked at the clock and saw it was only 6 o'clock in the morning. "Sweetie, I talked to the doctors down at the main campus and we are working on discharging you so that you can go and be with your baby", she said. *"Is she alright, is something wrong"*, I said anxiously. *"Everything is fine, I think they want to operate on her soon and we want you to go over and be with her. We had to order you a shot because you are RH Negative and your baby is positive. So, just as soon as that comes up, we can work on getting you out of here"*, she continued. *"Okay"*, I managed to get out as she left the room in a hurry.

Thomas arrived at the hospital to get me at about 10am. The OB doctor on call came in and went over all the guidelines she had me agree to follow as apart of her discharging me so early. She told me that my blood pressure was good and that she wanted me to sit down as much as I could. Outside of lifting the baby, she said for me to lift nothing. She told me to sit a chair next to my baby's bed and do nothing but sit. She also told me to pay close attention to my bleeding for it would let me know if I was being too active. A social worker down at the main campus called me on my phone and told me that she set us up with a room at the Ronald McDonald House. The Ronald McDonald House is a non-profit organization that helps the families of children with special needs. They only had one room left and the social worker was able to book it for us. I couldn't thank her enough; as I was just grateful to be close to Brielle and the hospital she was in, by any means possible.

In hindsight, I was appreciative that I listened to God. If I had gotten that epidural, it would've slowed my dilating down and, if I would've still ran into trouble like I did after her stool started coming out in my water, I would've needed a C-Section. If I would've gotten a C-Section, there was no way that I would've been able to get discharged from the hospital so that I could be with Brielle for her surgery.

The doctors at the main campus told us they were planning to take Brielle into surgery later that evening at 5pm. We found ourselves in a big hurry because we had to leave the first hospital, go and check in at The Ronald McDonald House, which sat right across the street from the second hospital, and then get to Brielle for her surgery. In the back of my mind, I was hoping that the report would change at the last minute so we wouldn't have to go through with the procedure. And while I practically begged the Lord to not let the surgery happen, God had another plan.

When Thomas and I arrived on the NICU floor, we had to check in at a security desk where we were required to show our ID. From there, they made us these special name tags that we had to wear on our shirts in order to see Brielle. The name tags were only good for one day so we were required to show our ID and get new name tags each day we visited. I understand it was for her protection but it was honestly a pain; especially if you forgot you're identification. Next, we had to scrub our hands and arms really well at this large

- 183 -

sink that sat next to yet another desk you needed to check in at to get to her actual room.

The floor was really pleasant and clean. The nurses were extremely friendly, which was really a big help during such a tough time. I was still unable to walk that well and was tremendously sore, so I was really thankful that Thomas pushed me around the hospital the entire time in a wheelchair. As he pushed me to Brielle's room, I noticed there were about four babies each in the other rooms. It was really sad seeing so many fragile and ill children. Some were on ventilators, some were so small that they lay in incubators covered completely with large blankets to give them the effect of being in their mother's womb; others were snuggled in their parent's arms whose sadness drew you into their eyes as they stared at you through the large windows of the rooms. With each passing room, I became more uneasy of what it would be like when I saw my own baby.

We had finally arrived at Brielle's room and every ounce of anxiety had now turned to excitement. "Look who's here Brielle", Thomas sang as he wheeled me in the room. "Hey Mommy's girl", I said as I stroked her face with my fingers. "I missed you so much", I continued. Brielle looked up at me bright-eyed, moving her arms and legs in response to both of our voices. Moments later, Minister Wells walked into the room and greeted us with big hugs and comfort. We had asked him to come down and cover Brielle before she went into surgery. Minister Wells blessed all of our heads with oil and we began to pray.

*How do you stand on the Word of God
when your legs of FAITH are Broken?*

Brandy "BrandyWine" Rankins

He Kept His Promise;

Scott then arrived and my husband provided us reassurance with a Word from God; he pulled out his Bible and both he and Scott began sharing Acts 27. From what I understood, there was a ship filled with a total of 276 men, one of who was Paul. Their boat had faced fourteen days worth of storms, terrible wind, and other struggles as they set sail for Italy. In addition to the storm they faced, they were also extremely hungry because they were fasting the entire fourteen days. They were trying to leave the ship but Paul advised them against it, telling them they would not only be met with disaster but would lose their lives also. Unfortunately, the centurion didn't pay much attention to him and continued toward the adversity. At one point, the storm really hit them hard and they had given up all hope of surviving it. Some of the sailors were even planning on sneaking out of the ship by way of a small boat; but Paul told them, unless all the men remain in the ship, everyone would die. So they ate; giving thanks to God, endured the storm, and made it out fine.

Ultimately, after they read the story, my husband began telling me that the only way out of the storm with Brielle was to go through it. He said, though the strong winds would blow and it may become dangerous to sail just like it was for Paul and the men, we couldn't abandon the boat. "*Bae, I know you are covered in fear and worry but we have to trust God*", he said. "*So we are gonna have to ride this thing until the wheels fall off, even if it seems like tragedy is near, because Brielle will come out victorious in Jesus' name*", he continued. "*Victorious in Jesus' name*", Scott repeated. "**In Jesus' name**", I followed.

- 185 -

"Hello Mr. and Mrs. Rankins", the surgeon said sharply as he entered the room. He pulled up a chair and began to go over his plan to operate on Brielle. "We expect the surgery to be about four hours", he said. "Four hours!!!" my lips dramatically moved without sound. The surgeon put his hand on my shoulder, smiled, and said "yeah, four hours mom. I am going to go in and try to cut out the areas of blockage and connect her intestines back together. I don't want to have to give her an ostomy bag; however, I won't know how extensive the damage is until I get in there". He further went on to explain to us what an ostomy bag is and how she would be put on the ventilator during the surgery. He said, more than likely, she would return back to the floor with the ventilator, depending how extensive her incisions and pain was. At the end of the conversation, he had three different surgery scenarios that would vary based on what he saw once he got inside. My resistance and worry was worn distinctly on my face as I tried to ingest all of what he was saying, as well as try to remember the right questions to ask. "Mrs. Rankins, I understand your worry and I want you both to know that I am a father myself. I'm married and we have a young child also. Honestly, if anything like this were to ever happen to him, I would bring him here to my colleagues and gladly let them operate; I trust them. We've been doing these kinds of surgeries for many years and I want you to know this is what we specialize in. This is not the first situation like this that we have dealt with. I'm going to take the best care of your little girl and try to help fix this the best way I can. You all have nothing wrong, this is just the hand nature dealt us, so now we have to do the best we can with it", he said. He placed his hands on both of our shoulders and we both nodded and said "thank you".

The surgery team arrived moments later and they greeted us with friendly smiles; then they began grabbing Brielle's chart and breaking her bed down, while explaining they were going to wheel her to surgery. One of them handed me a gown and told me that only one of us would be allowed to go into the Operating Room before they started to give her a kiss. While I was thankful, I felt like fainting from disbelief; the moment had actually arrived for her to have her surgery. My eyes welted with big tears as I just stopped and stared at Brielle, who was laying there cooing and actively playing. I fought hard to keep the tears inside while the moment continued feeling surreal. I put on the yellow gown and Thomas and I followed behind Brielle and the operating team, who were covered completely in blue masks and gowns, to the operating room.

*How do you stand on the Word of God
when your legs of FAITH are Broken?*

Brandy "BrandyWine" Rankins

He Kept His Promise;

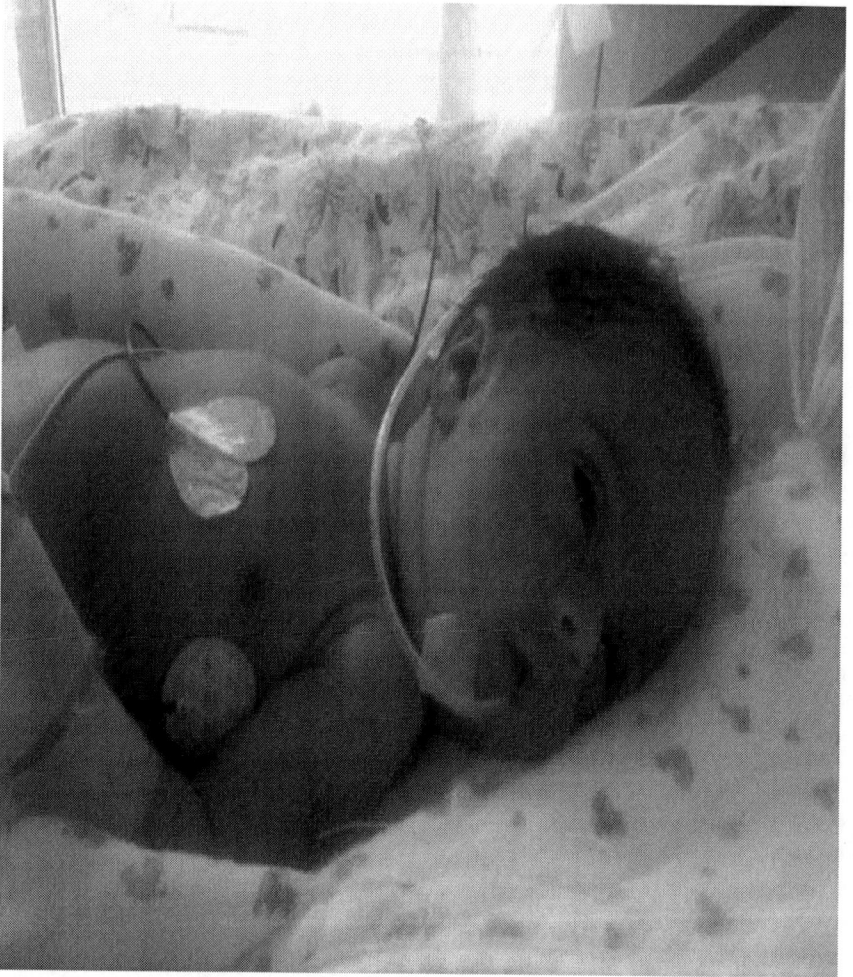

- 188 -

*How do you stand on the Word of God
when your legs of FAITH are Broken?*

Brandy "BrandyWine" Rankins

It's not a setback, God is setting you up for your miracle

{Chapter Twenty-Two}

*How do you stand on the Word of God
when your legs of FAITH are Broken?*

Brandy "BrandyWine" Rankins

We were instructed to wait in the family room because this is where we would receive surgery updates via phone calls. As we waited, I was glad to see Shaun come walking through the door. She greeted me with a huge hug and then sat down beside me. Next, Ida came through the door. Instantly, I smiled hard and shouted a friendly "hey" when I saw her because it meant a lot to me that she came.

Ida and her husband Mike (both are known as Minister Wells) are very good friends of ours. They have always gone beyond the call of duty to stand in our corner and show their unconditional love for our family. Again, her husband is who took the photos for our wedding and went out his way to provide us with exceptional quality pictures, even when many of them failed to print correctly. He and his wife also literally stayed up all night helping us with my mother's obituary, housed and fed us several nights leading up to my mother's passing, and, most of all, they've always done it all with a smile.

"Hey snookey", Ida said as she bent over to where I was sitting to give me a kiss. Ida has always been a big sister to me, so I was in no way surprised to see that she had a big black bag with her that had many goodies in it for me. When I opened it, I saw that it was filled with an elegant night gown, some t-shirts, shorts, toothpaste, toothbrush, deodorant, undergarments, and much more. I just felt so blessed that she cared so much to be so thoughtful; but that's just who Ida is and I love her. Following that, Lady Linda, Minister Darnell Jennings, and James came walking in.

It was so good to see everyone and receive their support at a time when we truly needed it most.

About three hours had passed by before we received the first call from the OR. They said that everything was going good and Brielle was responding well. While I felt really relieved to get the call, I just couldn't wait for the entire surgery to be over. God making all of our friends available to be with us helped tremendously because we were able to talk without completely focusing on what was taking place.

It had now been five hours and I was starting to get worried as I began pacing the room back and forth. "Come and sit down Bran, I'm sure everything is okay and you still need to rest yourself", Shaun said. Ida and Lady Linda joined in agreement. I tried munching on some of the snacks they had in the family room but I was too restless to eat. It was already after 11pm and I couldn't help but wonder what was taking so long.

Just when our wait turned into six hours, the phone rang. "Hello", I answered out of breath from running to the phone. "Is this the Rankins' family?" the nurse asked. "Yes", I said almost immediately. "We're done, the surgery went well, and the surgeon will be up shortly to speak with you", she finished. I told everyone what she said and we all smiled in relief that the surgery was not only over but went well. We all walked into the hallway as it was extremely late and everyone needed to leave. We walked them to the elevator and thanked them all for being there.

- 191 -

How do you stand on the Word of God
when your legs of FAITH are Broken?

Brandy "BrandyWine" Rankins

We spotted the surgeon coming off the elevator and he signaled for us to go into a conference room so that he could speak to us. He told us that the surgery went well but Brielle's intestines had really been affected by the blockage. He said that, once he removed the areas of blockage, reconnecting her large and small intestines was extremely challenging; "like connecting a garden hose to a spaghetti noodle", he stated. That's how much of a difference in her intestines the blockage had caused. He said that her large intestines were severely dilated (stretched out) from working so hard to get the bowel to move and that her small intestines were almost micro-sized because the blockage had shut off the blood supply to it. He stated that her colon was also micro-size and that he had to remove her appendix. There is also an intestinal disease that can cause such a blockage, so he told us he had sent off some samples to ensure that it wasn't that particular illness. He also said, in his medical opinion, he was sure that it wasn't the disease because she showed none of the symptoms; however, he wanted to test and be sure.

"We usually see this type of blockage in babies who mom's use crack cocaine", the surgeon said. My mouth fell completely open; yet before it could slap the floor he continued to say "however, we know that's totally not the case with you because of your blood work and history". "Naw I don't use drugs", I responded in disbelief. "I know, I know. I just have to run it all down to you. I can't say enough that this wasn't caused by anything that either of you did...it was just a bad stroke of luck and the hand that Mother Nature dealt us", he continued. "Don't be frightened by all the tubes when you go in there to see her. She's still on the ventilator because they are

How do you stand on the Word of God when your legs of FAITH are Broken?

Brandy "BrandyWine" Rankins

administering a high dosage of pain meds. She has a catheter for urine, and she has a Broviac catheter that we put in right up underneath the skin in her thigh that is held by a stitch. We put that in so she could receive the synthetic nutrition called TPN. This allows her to eat by vein since she isn't able to eat by mouth", he said. From there, he explained they were going to allow her to heal from the surgery and wait several days to see if she produced a bowel movement. If she did, great and we could move forth but, if she didn't, we might have to explore another surgery, something I didn't even want to think about. Thomas and I left the conference room and began preparing to go and see Brielle. We washed our hands at the large sink, checked in at the NICU desk, and waited to be buzzed back through the security door.

When we got to Brielle's room, words can't even describe how I felt seeing my baby connected to all of the monitors and tubes. The only thing I wanted to do was comfort her, and I didn't really know how to do that. However, the excitement and gratefulness I had toward God for her just being alive and okay immediately put me past what I saw with my natural eyes.

"Hey Mommy's girl", I said softly as I moved in closer to her face to let her know I was right there with her. "Hey Daddy's Doodlum", Thomas said, giving her that nickname because the blockage was relatively close to her Duodenum, a part of the intestines. It was becoming extremely late, so we stayed by her side for about another hour before going across the street to our room at The Ronald McDonald House to get some rest.

*How do you stand on the Word of God
when your legs of FAITH are Broken?*

Brandy "BrandyWine" Rankins

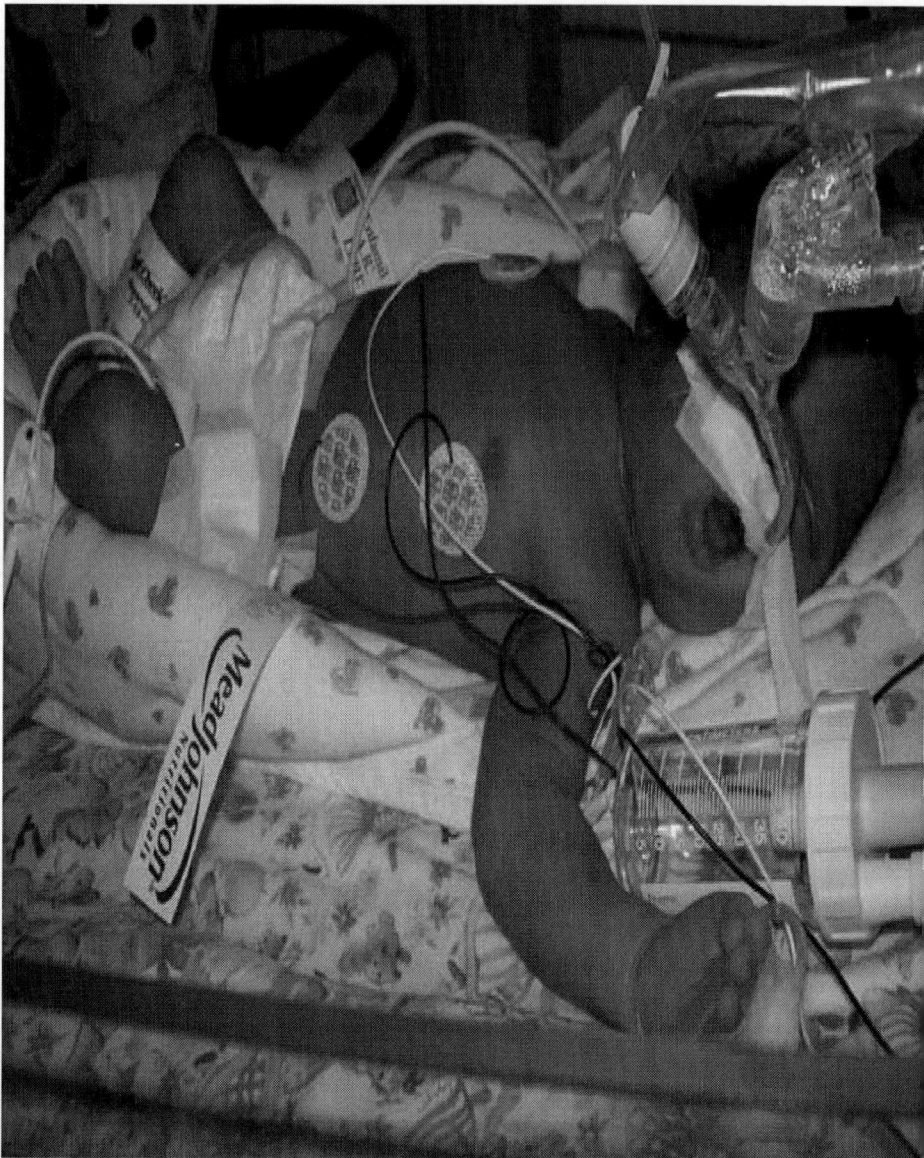

- 194 -

How do you stand on the Word of God
when your legs of FAITH are Broken?

Brandy "BrandyWine" Rankins

He Kept His Promise;

His GRACE Kept ME

{Chapter Twenty-Three}

- 195 -

*How do you stand on the Word of God
when your legs of FAITH are Broken?*

Brandy "BrandyWine" Rankins

He Kept His Promise;

About eight days had passed by and Brielle still was unable to have a bowel movement. Immediately I began posting pictures and Bible scriptures on her incubator and all around her room. She was taken off the ventilator a few days prior and most of the swelling had gone down from the large incision that completely covered her stomach and sealed together by stitches. I immediately went into prayer asking God not to allow her little fragile body to have to get cut on anymore. Thomas and Scott also went on a fast to pray against another surgery.

When the next day arrived, I spent most of the morning calling the nurses' station to the floor Brielle was on making inquiries. Whenever I wasn't at the hospital, I made it a habit to call and see how she was doing.   I was intensely in prayer about her not needing another surgery so my initial question was always "did Brielle have a bowel movement yet?" "No, Mrs. Rankins. I'm sorry, but she hasn't had one yet", they replied gently, as if I wasn't testing their patience from the last time I had called; despite it being literally five minutes ago.   I asked if there was any new news about Brielle needing surgery and the nurse told me that the doctors had already made their rounds and said she didn't need another procedure. Immediately, I was relieved and, for the first time since her birth, I didn't feel rushed in getting to the hospital. I decided to lie back down and get a few more hours of rest before heading over to see Brielle.

When I got to the hospital, I was literally skipping down the hall to her room in joy that my baby didn't need another surgery. However, once I made it to her room, I was sitting in the chair five

- 196 -

How do you stand on the Word of God
when your legs of FAITH are Broken?

Brandy "BrandyWine" Rankins

minutes before I received an upsetting report. "*Mrs. Rankins, the surgeon has been trying to reach you. They want to take Brielle down for surgery today*", the nurse said. "Today?" I questioned frantically. "*I was told she no longer needed surgery*", I snapped as I felt myself beginning to lose my temper. Just then, the breastfeeding consultant came in. It seemed like she was always coming to talk to me at the wrong time; which unfortunately was every time I saw her. She was trying to encourage me about breastfeeding but it was so hard to breastfeed a baby that I hadn't been able to put to my breast. She was unable to tolerate feeds, so pumping milk and storing it for her seemed like a good idea, but not a timely one. Initially, I pumped about every three hours for her. I had so many bottles stored in the freezer for her that they had to give me an entirely different shelf so I would have more room. Then, the milk began to leave me and, no matter how much I pumped, it seemed nothing made a difference.

"Hi Brandy, how have you been doing with your pumping?" the breastfeeding consultant asked. At first, I just sat there in the chair holding Brielle and was filled with too much emotion to even answer her. "She's not okay', Brielle's nurse responded for me. "She just found out that her baby has to go back into surgery, so right now isn't a good time for that", she said kindly. The Breastfeeding consultant sent her apologies and then walked out the room. "Lord, I don't understand why you are allowing this to happen", I began sobbing as I sat in the chair. I felt like breaking out screaming at the top of my lungs; but I knew I couldn't because, once I started, I wouldn't stop, or they may kick me out the hospital. So I just sat there sobbing and talking to God. Just when I thought I was about to lose it, I got a page over the intercom in the room saying that my Pastor was upfront. They sent my Pastor, Bishop C. Wayne Brantley, to my room and, as much as I tried, I couldn't even pull it together before he entered. As I cried, I rocked Brielle in my arms and updated Pastor Brantley on everything that was going on. Immediately, he pulled out his oil and began speaking into my life. He told me that we don't always agree with what God is doing because our minds are unable to comprehend His divine plan. He also said he knew it had to be extremely hard to have my newborn baby undergo these surgeries, but at some point I had to trust God. I didn't even have to think about what he said before I received it because I knew he was right. His words gave me comfort, strength, and new clarity during one of the most chaotic times of my life. Pastor Brantley then anointed Brielle and me on our foreheads before we all looked to God in prayer. After we prayed, I thanked him; and that's when he turned to me and said what he always says to me during difficult times "WE ARE PRAYING FOR YOU AND THOMAS BOTH, AND REMEMBER...WE GOT YOU COVERED". My Pastor and First Lady have been at my side during some of the most troubling moments ever, like when my mother passed. Truly, there was something special about hearing him say "We got you covered" that let me know everything was going to be alright. I called Thomas at work and told him everything that was going on and he immediately left his job to be at our side.

Shortly after Thomas arrived to the hospital, we were told that the surgeon's last surgery had run over and he would be up to the room as soon as he could to talk to us. When the surgeon arrived,

How do you stand on the Word of God
when your legs of FAITH are Broken?

Brandy "BrandyWine" Rankins

he told us that he definitely needed to take Brielle back to surgery. He said that her still being unable to have a bowel movement could be extremely harmful. He explained how this could make her a candidate for infection or cause adhesions (sticking together of the intestines). He went on to say that he wanted to take her to surgery again immediately and that he would have to take a different approach this time. He said that he needed to form two ostomies on her stomach since she was unable to have a bowel movement through her rectum. From the ostomy on the large intestines, he would manually collect the stool through a syringe and push it through the other ostomy into the small intestine. He said the only way to get the small intestine to grow would be to feed bowel through it. He continued on to say that he wanted to take Brielle to surgery the next day at 2pm and how exhausted he was from his last surgery.

That was about all I was able to gather before I completely went numb with anger and disappointment from hearing Brielle still needed another surgery. Even up to that point, I hoped that God would reverse the report. While I knew she needed the surgery and all of the benefit that she would gain from having it, my mind somehow just kept getting stuck at "she needs another surgery". Just knowing that someone was literally going to take a knife to my fragile, precious baby was frightening and devastating. After meeting with the surgeon, Thomas and I stayed by Brielle's side for about another hour before exhaustion made us return to our room across the street.

- 199 -

He Kept His Promise;

The Ronald McDonald House was truly a blessing to our family. Just the convenience alone it provided to go back and forth across the street to see Brielle made a difference. There are different businesses, churches, and families that donate meals for the families who room there. They were really nice meals that were usually served buffet style; and so all of us, the boys included, always received more than enough to eat. They also had different activities there for the children throughout the week. One time, reps from the zoo came, bringing different animals for the children to hold and learn about. Jah'Mir especially was so excited when they pulled out the snake; he couldn't believe how big and long one of God's creatures could be. Then there were the other tenants who stayed there; truly it was humbling. We saw children with trach collars, some with missing body parts, malformations, cancer, sleeping disorders, brain conditions, and beyond; yet their parents were always smiling and trying to encourage and help me out when I was alone with the boys. Suddenly, all the loneliness I felt about the situation I was in began to fade away. By my husband Thomas being a paramedic and the only working body in our home, he worked twelve, sometimes fourteen hour days and every other weekend; so, many days I was at the Ronald McDonald House by myself with the boys, not yet healed but doing my best to get around. One of my sisters came by often to help and I also made some friends there as well.

There was Ashley for instance who had a daughter that had surgery to place a trach in her throat because she had feeding issues. Her daughter was three months older than Brielle and was at another hospital in the other direction, about ten minutes up the

- 200 -

*How do you stand on the Word of God
when your legs of FAITH are Broken?*

Brandy "BrandyWine" Rankins

street. Then, there was Danielle who gave birth to her first son when she was about twenty weeks pregnant. She told me that her baby literally could fit in the palm of her hand when she birthed him. She explained how, for the first few months, she was unable to hold him and could only look at him through the incubator that stayed covered with a blanket for most of the time. He was now six months old and had a lot of medical complications remaining from birth. He had cardiac hypertension; I think some liver issues, and much more. I immediately began encouraging both Ashley and Danielle and even went to pray with Danielle's baby on a few occasions. They in turn blessed me as well; keeping Braelyn and sometimes all the boys so that I could visit with Brielle.

The NICU did not let children under four years old on the unit to visit, so Braelyn was never allowed to visit with Brielle while she was there. This was extremely challenging on days Thomas worked because I had no one to watch Braelyn so that I could visit with Brielle. Many days I became very sad about this and sometimes even felt guilty because I was unable to see her. However, Thomas always stopped to see her whether or not he had a call in the area, so it comforted me to know she was frequently seeing at least one of us.

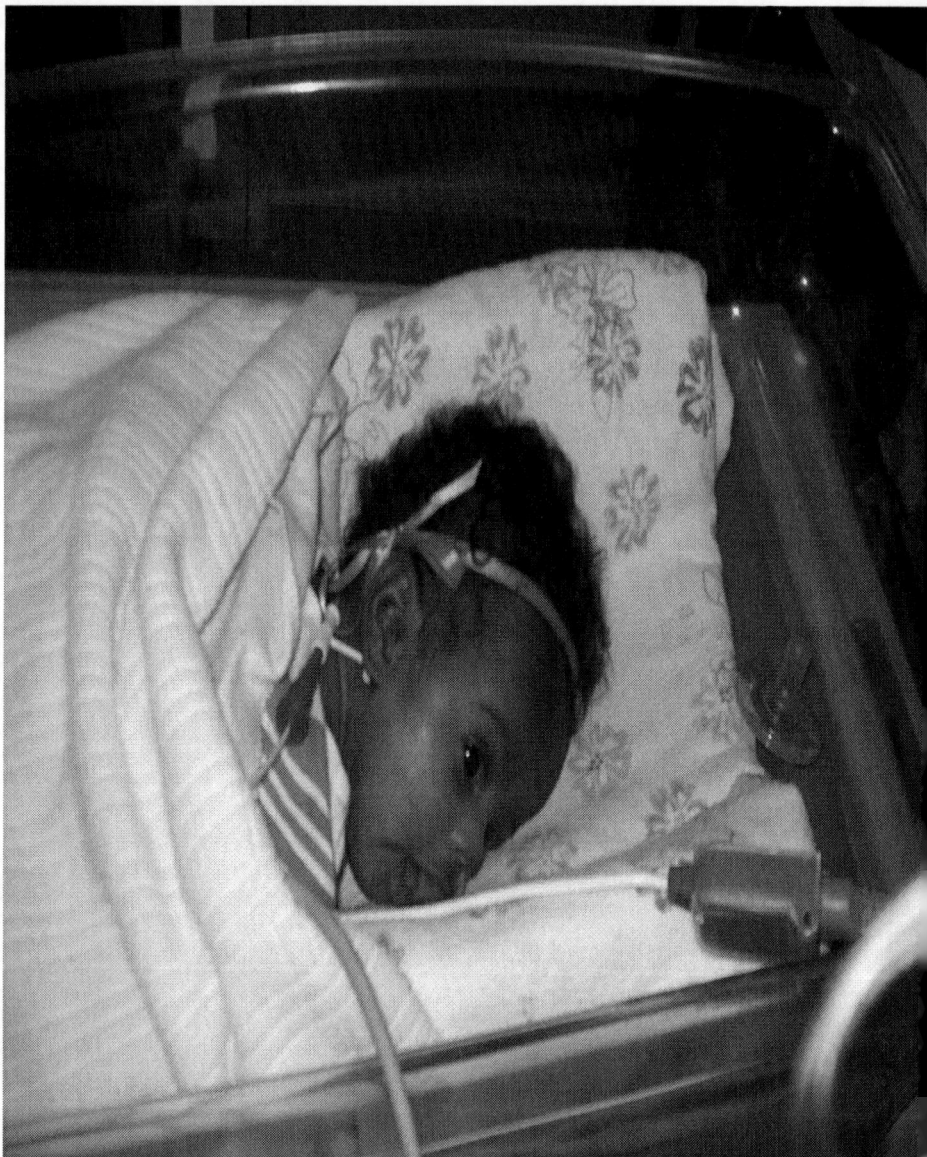

- 202 -

How do you stand on the Word of God
when your legs of FAITH are Broken?

Brandy "BrandyWine" Rankins

God will use YOU to minister to others in the midst of your storm

{Chapter 24}

He Kept His Promise;

The next day arrived and still I was dreading the thought of Brielle having another surgery. As I went downstairs to the kitchen of the Ronald McDonald House for a late breakfast, I was met by Danielle. She told me that her baby's doctor was saying that his heart wasn't pumping well and there was nothing else they could do. She asked me to come to the hospital and pray with him. At first, I told her that I couldn't because Brielle was scheduled for surgery and I wouldn't have enough time. However, when she started to walk away and leave, the Lord put a "go" in my spirit and so I called her back and told her yes.

As we rode together on the shuttle to the other hospital, I stayed in constant prayer. See, it was extremely challenging going to the hospital with Danielle; her son was at the same hospital my mom was at before she passed. The closer we got to the hospital, different emotions were trying to rise up against me but I just kept speaking the Word of God against them. I had my anointing oil in my pocket and I planned on dousing it on anything that wasn't in agreement with the Word.

When we arrived at her son's room in the NICU, there were many doctors around his bed. The atmosphere was filled with a deep heaviness and Danielle instantly fell out screaming and crying. The doctors just bowed their heads and her son was taking rapid breaths, followed by loud sounds of congestion. I too almost became covered in heaviness but I pushed my emotions aside and began singing to the Lord. At first, I had a hard time remembering the lyrics to some of the most basic gospel songs that I sang often, so I began making words up. Then, I pulled out my oil, blessed

- 204 -

How do you stand on the Word of God
when your legs of FAITH are Broken?

Brandy "BrandyWine" Rankins

everyone in the room, and in total faith, went into prayer believing God for the impossible.

When I was done praying, I spoke a few words of encouragement to Danielle and then dashed off to the other hospital to make Brielle's surgery. Thomas drove over to the hospital to meet me and was waiting downstairs in front. I literally ran through all the hallways, the lobby, and even exited the hospital running. I immediately jumped in the car with Thomas as smoke and screeching tires filled the streets as we hurried off.

Brielle's surgery lasted close to eight hours and it seemed like the phone calls to notify us of her status took forever to come in. I was both tired and excited when I heard they were finally done, and I couldn't wait to see her. When she was back in her room, all over again I became heartbroken seeing my baby plugged to so many tubes as I stood over her. She had three large flesh wounds, which were the ostomies, coming out of different areas of her stomach. One was to the left of her navel, the other to the right, and the final sat above it. They were covered with these large clear plastic like bags. In addition to the three ostomies, she was on the ventilator again, the catheter for urine, and the Broviac catheter was still in place. It just seemed like so much for a tiny baby to have to endure. I just felt so disappointed that God was allowing Brielle to go through this.

Thomas and I sat by her bed for hours. The hardest part was that we were told we couldn't touch

*How do you stand on the Word of God
when your legs of FAITH are Broken?*

Brandy "BrandyWine" Rankins

He Kept His Promise;

- 206 -

*How do you stand on the Word of God
when your legs of FAITH are Broken?*

Brandy "BrandyWine" Rankins

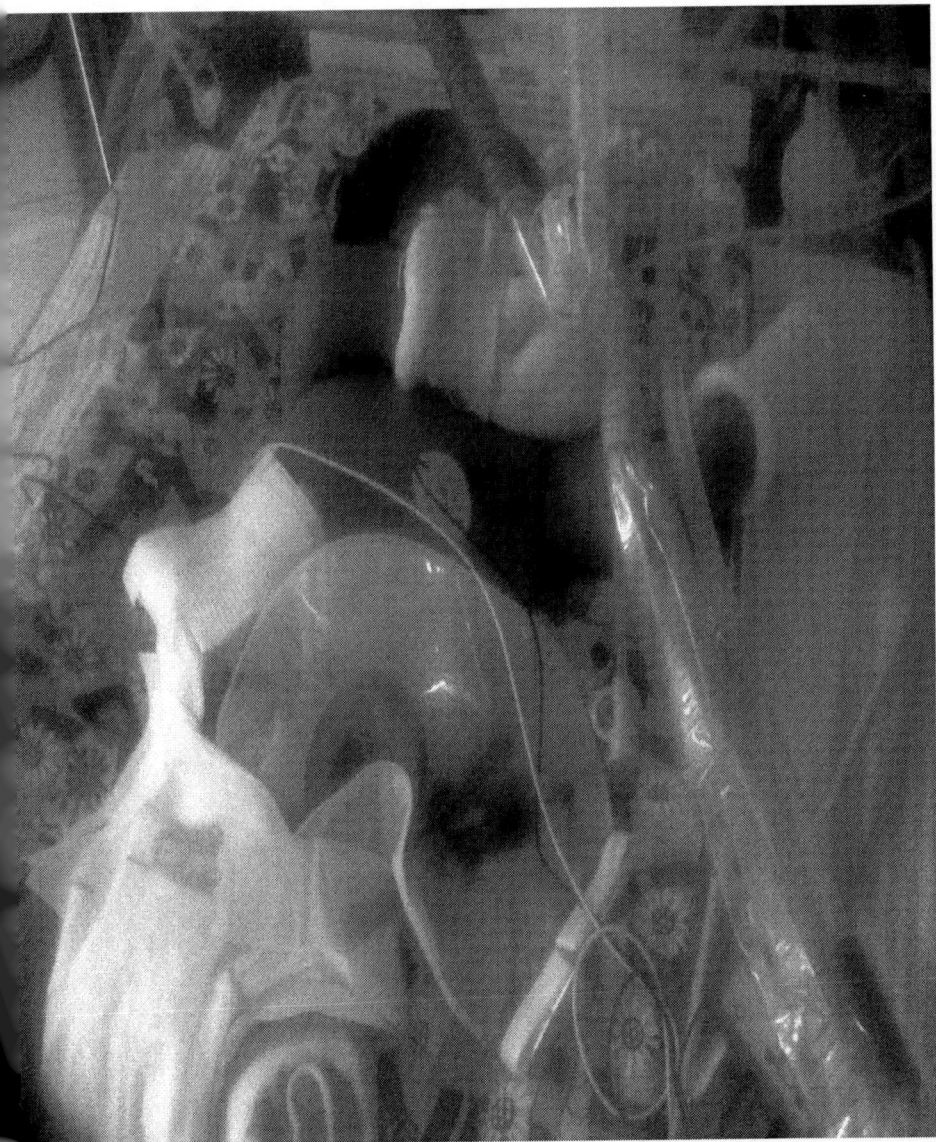

- 207 -

*How do you stand on the Word of God
when your legs of FAITH are Broken?*

Brandy "BrandyWine" Rankins

her because it may cause more pain. She grimaced a lot and, as the days progressed, she began breathing against the ventilator. This was extremely scary for me because she would look like she was choking; her eyes would bulge and she would wheeze as the machine pumped the air in and out of her. The nurses also told me that mucus could get caught in her chest and throat so they stuck this long suction tube into the ventilator and down her throat to remove it. I absolutely hated it and, like a three year old, I sat there with my arms folded having a temper tantrum with God about it. Of course, who would come walking in at the worst time possible? That's right...the breast feeding specialist. She came asking me if I had been pumping regularly and wanted to watch me pump to ensure I was doing it right. "Are you serious", I thought. "Lady, this is my third child and she's laying up right now plugged to a ventilator and can't even drink the milk, so if you don't go somewhere you better!!!!" I wanted to yell but I just smiled and went to the lactation room to fulfill her request.

"Where are you Lord because I just don't see you right now", I cried. "How could you be letting this happen, I just don't feel you anywhere? You said you would never leave or forsake us but it feels like you have", I continued. I got up from her bedside and just went into the family room and cried. I didn't just cry for Brielle but I cried for all the sick children, and just the sick period. I just wanted to help and make them all better but I couldn't.

As I sat in the family room wallowing in my tears, a woman came over to encourage me. She gave me a big hug and told me to trust God. To the left of her, sitting on the couch watching T.V, was her

How do you stand on the Word of God when your legs of FAITH are Broken?

Brandy "BrandyWine" Rankins

own daughter who couldn't have been more than fifteen. She was connected to an i.v., was in pajamas, and had alopecia. I thought maybe she had cancer but I didn't want to ask; I didn't want to deal with the response if the answer was yes.

About a week later, Brielle got off the ventilator. I was so excited to hold my baby. I covered her face with kisses and just thanked God for her. She was now able to have bowel movements through her ostomy bags and they allowed me to feed her milk from the bottles that I previously stored. Minutes after covering her face with kisses, she gave me the biggest smile. It was at the exact moment she smiled that I heard God speak to me. "You asked where I was but I have been right here with you all along", he said. "I was here praying by the bedside for you when you couldn't even find the words to pray for yourself", He said. Then, he showed me several visions of the hospital clergy who stood by Brielle's bedside with her hand on my shoulder praying us through. He showed me another vision of my good friend Shawana that came by and blessed us with twenty dollars so we could buy ourselves dinner. Then, He said "surely, I have been here with you this entire time giving you everything you need. And how could I allow Brielle to go through such a thing?" His voice echoed. "I created her especially to go through this. Her body may be afflicted but her spirit is untouched. I am showing you that right now in her smile. Despite the tubes, despite the surgeries, she is still smiling…in me she is victorious", He said, and then I cried. I apologized to God for ever doubting him; for not understanding His plan. The more and more I looked at Brielle, I realized God was right, her spirit was untouched and I believed everything would be alright.

How do you stand on the Word of God when your legs of FAITH are Broken?

Brandy "BrandyWine" Rankins

Brielle kept the ostomies for about two months. Her small intestines grew immensely from all of the manual bowel feeds. At one point, Brielle became extremely ill; a high fever and unable to hold feedings. Her doctors were very concerned about the chance of her having an infection, so they gave a complete workup which included a spinal tap. When they told us they wanted to perform a spinal tap, we disagreed because we didn't want to put Brielle through any additional pain, especially if it was unnecessary. However, when her fever continued to elevate and wouldn't break, we agreed to let them do it. They explained to us that doing a spinal tap was essential to ensure Brielle didn't have meningitis. The handling of stool around her, as well as manually inserting it into her intestines, along with her simply being a patient in the hospital, put her at risk. In the end, Brielle thankfully did not have meningitis, but instead a bladder infection and a bad reaction to the immunizations she was given just days prior. She was treated with antibiotics, and within a week she felt better and was able to eat again.

It wasn't long before we received the news that Brielle would undergo her final surgery to reconnect all of the ostomies in her intestines back together. While I still wasn't happy at the thought of her undergoing surgery a third time, I was really excited about her having everything reconnected so that we could go home and live a normal life. The surgeon told us that, if her surgery went well, she should still be able to tolerate full feeds and go home within two weeks. I couldn't wait for Brielle to come home, so on the weekends following her surgery, I began going home and getting her room ready.

How do you stand on the Word of God
when your legs of FAITH are Broken?

Brandy "BrandyWine" Rankins

Brielle underwent her third and final surgery. It lasted for about five hours and she was placed on the ventilator a last time. Within six days, Brielle was off the ventilator and was ready to eat. Unfortunately, my milk was nearly depleted and I was unable to provide enough for her total nutrition. They tried several different types of milk on Brielle until they reached the one that was broken down enough for her to tolerate. Now, the real test had come, for it was time to feed Brielle and watch her bowels go to work!

How do you stand on the Word of God
when your legs of FAITH are Broken?

Brandy "BrandyWine" Rankins

He Kept His Promise;

How do you stand on the Word of God
when your legs of FAITH are Broken?

Brandy "BrandyWine" Rankins

"If God allows You to be publicly Crucified, He will also allow you to be publicly Resurrected"

{Chapter 25}

How do you stand on the Word of God when your legs of FAITH are Broken?

Brandy "BrandyWine" Rankins

Miraculously, Brielle's bowels were working, however, she was unable to tolerate full feeds through a bottle without it causing excessive diarrhea. She was still receiving the TPN but it was causing her liver levels to become high. They would feed her only like 10 mls of milk every two to three hours and instantly it would cause the diarrhea. I couldn't understand how, before she had her final surgery, she was up to like 40 mls of milk and was tolerating it well but was unable to tolerate it now. Her surgeon repeatedly explained to us that her intestines had help with the ostomies and now they would have to do all the work by themselves.

A few weeks passed without much increase in her oral feeds and her surgeon began thinking that it might be months before she could tolerate full feeds. He suggested that she could come home, but would need extensive in-home nursing to not only handle her medical equipment, but monitor her third shift to make certain she didn't pull out her NG tube and aspirate. An NG tube is a tube that runs through your nose and down to the opening of your stomach for liquid feedings. She received a continuous feed of her milk through the NG, which means she received a very small amount around the clock. In addition to the continuous feeds, she also received tiny bottle feedings (1 tablespoon) to ensure she didn't lose her natural swallowing instincts.

How do you stand on the Word of God
when your legs of FAITH are Broken?

Brandy "BrandyWine" Rankins

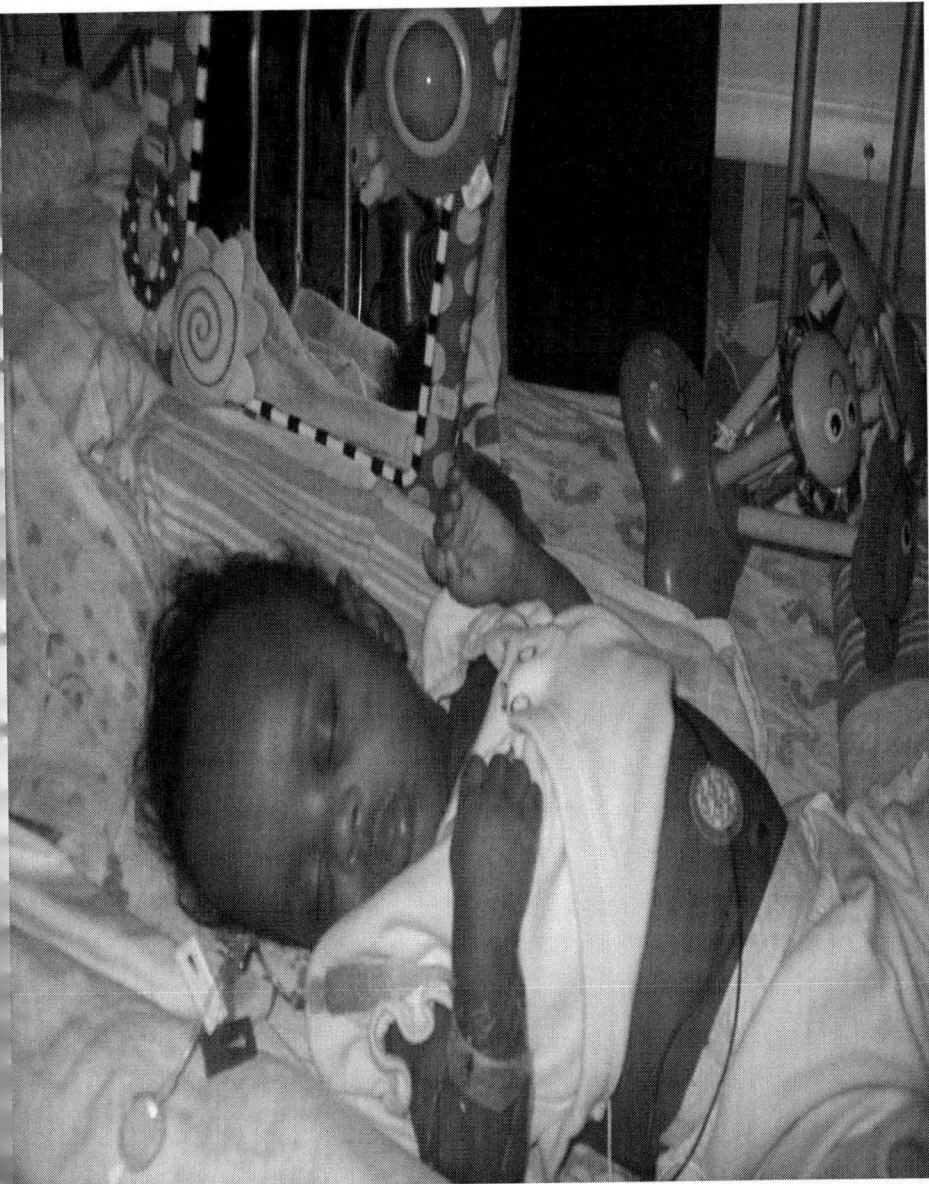

- 215 -

*How do you stand on the Word of God
when your legs of FAITH are Broken?*

Brandy "BrandyWine" Rankins

The other option was to place Brielle in a children's rehabilitation center where they would care for her until she was able to tolerate the full feeds. Both choices seemed to be complicated and, before I knew it, I stressed myself completely out about it and had to be put on blood pressure medicine. The thought of having to care for Brielle with all the medical equipment at home, with three other small children, made me extremely nervous and I began having panic attacks. I was concerned that my one year old might accidentally pull out one of her tubes because he was at that exploring stage and touched everything; especially the things you told him not to. Also if I brought her home, one of the biggest challenges I would've had to overcome was changing her NG tube. This meant I would've had to manually stick the tube properly into her nose and all the way down her throat, to the opening of stomach. While there weren't too many things that made me queasy, this did. I saw nurses change Brielle's NG tube plenty of times however, Brielle always gagged from its insertion and I always sat there beside her gagging too. On the other hand, I felt guilty for putting her in a rehab center and just wanted the entire ordeal to be over already.

Finally, after discussing all of the details, Thomas and I agreed to put her in the children's rehab because we couldn't afford to have him stay home from work without pay, and we also didn't think it was wise for me to try and take care of her special needs with three other small children all over the place. She spent a total of three months in the NICU and an additional four months in rehab. During those four months, it was an emotional rollercoaster, as they tried many different methods to get Brielle to full feeds. The most

How do you stand on the Word of God
when your legs of FAITH are Broken?

Brandy "BrandyWine" Rankins

significant symptoms Brielle showed to let us know that she was unable to tolerate the feed increase were projectile vomiting and excessive diarrhea. When this would happen, the doctors would completely cut off Brielle's feeds for about eight hours or more, depending on how sick she was, to keep her from dehydrating. Since her feeds were so inconsistent like this for many months, it became common for her to be very underweight as well. Her feeding inconsistencies also affected her nutrition and head growth, and caused worry at times for everyone.

In one instance, she caught a virus and had to be rushed back to the main campus where she was kept for a week before being transported back to the rehab. It seemed like the slightest little cold or infection made Brielle extremely sick, and that made her doctors uneasy. They began adding contact restrictions and quarantining her to her room if someone on the floor had a cold as well.

About the same time Brielle was placed into the children's rehab, Jah'Mir started kindergarten and we were no longer able to stay at The Ronald McDonald House because of the distance. Going back home without Brielle was extremely difficult and depression tried to show its ugly head. It was a constant battle mentally because I refused to succumb to it. Whenever I was away from her, I called the hospital to frequently check on her and I knew my other children were starving for my attention and time as well. Sometimes I felt guilty even for the short periods I was away from Brielle to take care of necessary things. It became a lot easier to make frequent visits to her because Braelyn was allowed to visit her at the rehab whereas at the NICU he wasn't because he was so young. This especially made Braelyn happy because no he could go and see this baby sister of his everybody was always talking so much about.

Because of what we were dealing with Brielle along with other things on our plate, we tried making any and everything we did with the kid's fun. Thomas was wonderful in this area. One time we went shopping at the store and when I looked down the toy aisle, I was surprised to see them dressed as baseball players. Thomas had them pretend to throw balls and forth to him and he ran up and down the aisles pretending to catch them. Many people not only stopped and smiled but they took special notice to the loud laughter coming from our children. I too took special notice to their laughter and for the first time since Brielle's birth I didn't feel guilty at all for having such a good time with the other kids. We also took the kids to a local amusement park; they loved it. There were animals from the zoo there and I was shocked at how well they touched the snakes, turtles, and spiders; I wouldn't dare touch the spider!

I really admire my children and how well they were enduring Brielle's long hospital stay. We knew it had to be a lot for them to sacrifice their entire summer between the hospital, the Ronald McDonald House, and now the new rehab; especially with them being so small. I especially apologized to them because during that time I was extremely on edge, always snapping and fussing, and just angry most of the time. I explained to them I was this way not because of them but because of the hard time we were facing with Brielle. I always reassured them that she would be home soon and I encouraged them to lay hands on her and say as many prayers

How do you stand on the Word of God
when your legs of FAITH are Broken?

Brandy "BrandyWine" Rankins

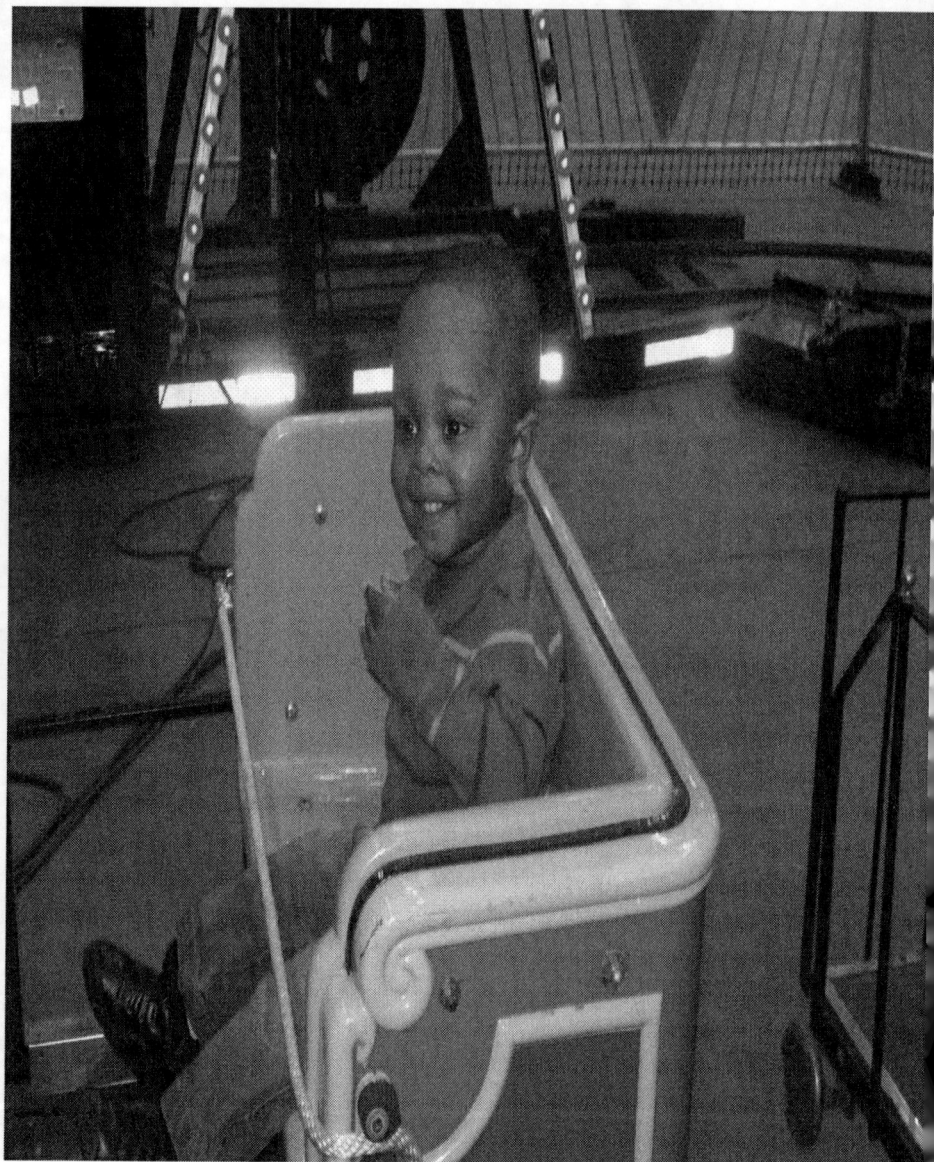

How do you stand on the Word of God
when your legs of FAITH are Broken?

Brandy "BrandyWine" Rankins

How do you stand on the Word of God
when your legs of FAITH are Broken?

Brandy "BrandyWine" Rankins

- 222 -

How do you stand on the Word of God
when your legs of FAITH are Broken?

Brandy "BrandyWine" Rankins

over her, when they visited her, as they could. I know this not only made them feel good but it also reiterated to them how important their roles were in her life as big brothers.

Brielle underwent many types of therapy while she was a patient at the rehab. The doctors created an entire schedule where each day she was doing something. She would rotate between physical therapy, occupational therapy, musical therapy, recreational therapy, dieticians, etc. The social worker there was named Kelly and she was especially nice to our family. She always came by to say hi, see how we were doing, and she always made sure I had enough free food vouchers to feed the children and toys in our room for them to play with. She even would take Braelyn and Toma'rez with her on ten and fifteen minute walks so that I could have some alone time with Brielle. I especially appreciated that because Thomas was the only working and his days consisted of 12-14 shifts. So the responsibility of the kids mainly rested on me and I didn't get many breaks. So for God to give a total stranger compassion for my family in a way that made them want to help out, was really was a big blessing.

One thing I liked about Brielle being in the rehab was there was always a plan in place for her to go home. Each week we met with the entire team that cared for her and discussed what milestones she needed to reach in order to go home. Not only did the team list their goals but Thomas and I listed ours as well. One thing we had to submit to was learning how to put in and take out her NG tube. "Oh no not that ", I thought as I felt myself becoming nauseous. And really the only one who needed to submit to it was me because

Thomas is a paramedic and didn't think twice about inserting tube in Brielle or anything else. The doctors told us not only did we have to learn how to insert the tube but we had to show them that we could do it as well before Brielle could come home.

There was no question that I desperately wanted Brielle to come home. For months I had struggled with even thinking about inserting a NG tube but when I measured it being the difference in whether or not she would come home...I immediately surrendered and said I would learn.

The nurse trained Thomas and I different times at throughout the week on how to insert the tube. Thomas had no problem learning and I knew he wouldn't and please believe he had no problem gloating about. Once he was done, he would hold the tube out over the doll, who was our patient, and shake it at me with a sneaky grin on his face. "Show off", I said before rolling my eyes, dramatically snapping my neck in laughter, and stepping up to the plate. The nurse showed us how to measure the tube before inserting it. We had to start the tube, with one hand, from the tip of her nose and with our other hand tightly run the tube down to her stomach and measure it. Once we identified the point of measurement, we marked it with a marker. From there we inserted it into her nostril, fed it down into her stomach, and then tape the small part that we didn't feed in, to the side of her nose. It would then look like the picture on the opposite page. "Don't we need to lubricate this?" I said. Before the nurse could answer I said "And can't she choke on this tube, it's so long and thick?" The nurse tried to speak and then I interjected "And how do we *really* know this doesn't hurt her? It's not like she can talk or tell us", I said sarcastically with my hand on

He Kept His Promise;

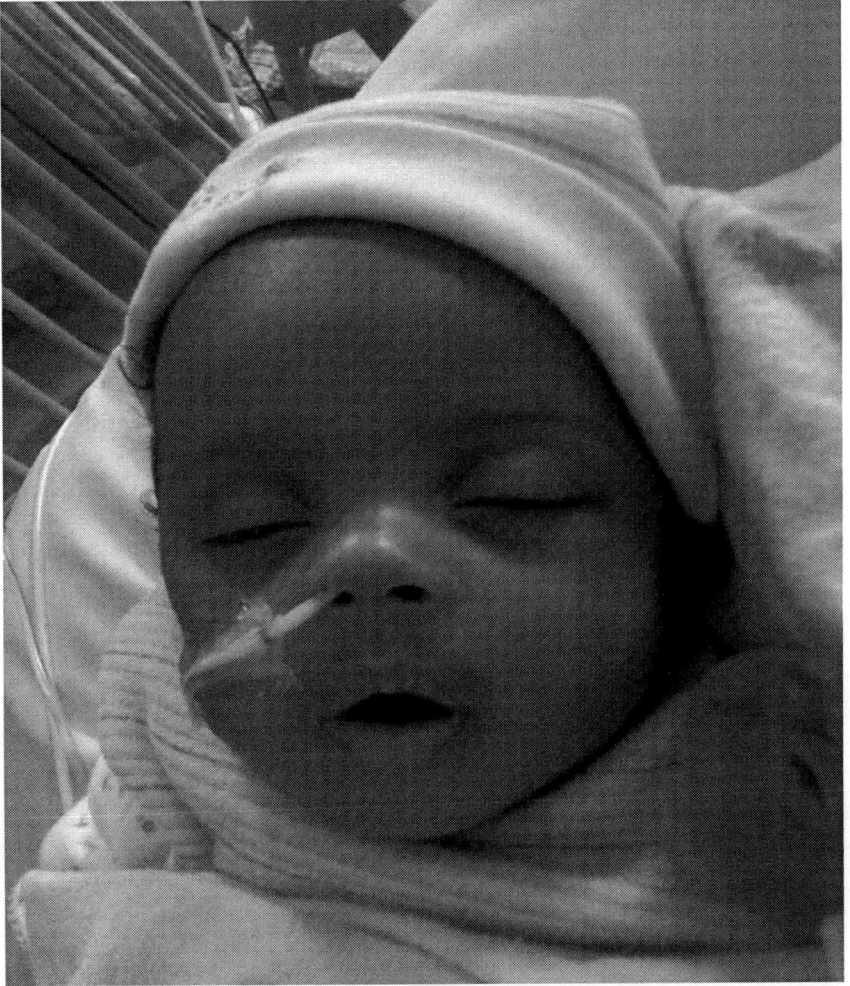

- 225 -

How do you stand on the Word of God
when your legs of FAITH are Broken?

Brandy "BrandyWine" Rankins

my hip. "*It always looks like it hurts her to me*", I scoffed. The nurse took a big sigh and let out a nervous grin and I knew in the back of her mind she had some choice words for me. My husband loudly cleared his throat and I made sure to only use my peripheral vision to look at him; standing there with his mouth turned up, staring at me with a dirty look. When I finally made eye contact with him, he nodded his head and I made an annoying face and stuck my tongue out at him before we both busted out laughing. My husband knew I was extremely protective, especially of the children and if something didn't look right to me, I was speaking out about it.

Soon it was the election day of November 2008. Thomas and I explained to the children the importance of voting and how as African American we haven't always had that right; so it was important to go and vote. We also explained to them the importance of letting your voice being heard despite which person won. Later that night we all sat around the television as we witness history take place. Barack Obama was the first African person elected as President of the United States. It was a wonderful moment for many, us included, and I believe it will be a historic event that will be remembered for many generations to come.

Before long, Thanksgiving, Christmas, and New Years came and went; and we were right there by Brielle's side to spend every single holiday. There were many church ministries and families that came and made donations throughout the holidays. For example, there was one family, whose children were perfectly healthy, that brought a movie, pizza, popcorn, and a lot of candy for the kids during Christmas. They showed the movie on a big screen in a conference room that seated many. I was completely humbled as I watched several of the children with illnesses put some of the biggest smiles upon their faces as they watched with their families. The best part was holding Brielle in my arms while her father and three brothers smiled as they surrounded her. Hands down, that was the best movie, even unto this day, that my family has ever seen.

The kids were used to spending the night at the rehab; especially on the weekends. Jah`Mir was in kindergarten, so I had a routine down where the other kids and I would drop him off at the bus stop and then, from the time school began until he got out, we stayed with Brielle. Toma'rez was four years old and Braelyn was one and half. Despite it being the middle of winter and very cold, they loved bundling up and going to spend time with their sister. We would make pallets on the floor and even purchased an air mattress to accommodate our entire family, three children and two adults, while Brielle slept in her hospital bed. The whole experience made us so much more grateful and thankful for Brielle.

Brielle was getting older and stronger and she was always good for pulling out her tubes. The Broviac catheter that was surgically placed into her thigh had broken right before she came to rehab. Once they explained putting a new one in meant taking her back to surgery...I said no. It turned out later that she didn't need it for her tolerance for milk began to increase. Brielle also pulled out her NG tube often. The doctors at the rehab didn't believe she could handle total bottle feeds without becoming in so they also reinserted it and kept it in place. When Brielle caught a fever, and was transported back to main campus to be examined, she was admitted for two days. Those doctors decided not to put in her NG tube and allowed her to drink solely from the bottle. Brielle tolerated the feeds just fine and when she returned back to rehab on that third day, the real test came. It was great that for those two days she drank and tolerated full feeds from a bottle but what about long term? Would she be able to handle it? Guess what? She did and the NG tube was no more.

I think the biggest lesson behind the NG tube was it seemed to be the worst thing in my mind but God wanted to know would I do whatever He asked me to do no matter how I felt about it. Once I gave a "yes" in my spirit, I was no longer nauseous or stressed out by the thought of it. Instead I was able to laugh about it and most of all conquer the skill that I didn't believe I could.

When Brielle turned seven months, my husband shared with me a Word he had received from the Lord about the number seven. He said that, although he was aware the number indicated completion, God sent him to go and get a more elaborate interpretation. He was led to a website that said the number seven means ENOUGH and that the job was done, the purpose was fulfilled, and that as much as necessary has taken place. My husband told me that God said, pertaining to Brielle; the time had come where it was ENOUGH. Weeks prior to Brielle turning seven months, she pulled out the catheter she was receiving TPN in and I refused to have her undergo another surgery to have it replaced. Initially, the doctors hesitated to go forth without the TPN, but they did...and you know what? Brielle tolerated it. Then, she pulled out her NG tube, which she had done many, many times in the past, but this time, instead of inserting back into her nose, the main campus left it out.

My husband then shared with me a story in the Bible where God gave Moses and His people land but they had to go and possess it. Thomas told me now was the time to go and possess Brielle and bring her home. We had weekly meetings with the doctors and we scheduled a meeting with them the next day. During these meetings, everyone who cared for Brielle was present; for instance her dietician was there, nurses, occupational and physical therapist, social worker, and the list went on and on. So in short, there were at least a good ten to fifteen people on hand when Thomas and I or I alone had these weekly meetings with them. At first, it was somewhat intimidating, but overtime I learned to listen to their thoughts as well as share mine firmly without giving it a second thought. Our meeting went like this:

"We would like to keep Brielle at the 50 mls of milk she is receiving and try to add a new regimen", the doctor said. *"I'm sorry to cut you off doctor. We appreciate everything that you all have done for our daughter these past four months but now its time for us to take her home"*, Thomas said. The room fell completely silent from shock. *"Well, I really don't think that's a good idea Mr. Rankins. You see, Brielle is still heavily under weight, her immune system is weak, and she still is not tolerating enough milk by mouth"*, the doctor replied. *"I really don't mean to be rude but we've decided we are taking Brielle home now and again, we thank you for everything"*, my husband said firmly. And needless to say, by

the end of the meeting, they were signing Brielle over to us and we were making arrangements to take her home.

It was the first week of January 2009, and the day had finally come to take Brielle home. I was awakened by a phone call at 6am from Lady Linda asking *"when are we going to get our baby?"* Unfortunately, that day had broken the weather record as being the coldest day of the winter in the last ten years. Although it was bone chilling cold outside, there was absolutely nothing that was going to keep me from getting my baby and bringing her home. I left the boys with a neighbor and my friend Kendra and I headed to the rehab to get Brielle. I met Kendra on a social network on the internet. I asked her to submit her testimony for my newsletter, The Redeemed Women of God, months earlier to encourage others. God has healed Kendra from MS (Multiple Sclerosis) and she tells her testimony every single chance she gets. She's a very friendly, humble, beautiful person, and I immediately felt like I knew her for years when I met her. *"I can't wait to meet the miracle baby"*, she proclaimed as we went to pick up Brielle.

When I arrived at the rehab, I was surprised to see that Lady Linda had beaten me there. It was one the nicest surprises ever to see her there. The other, was seeing my husband Thomas, who had to work, sneak away briefly so that he could be there when she was released. It was the greatest feeling ever...no words can even explain it. When we all made it to Brielle's room, she was bouncing up and down and cooing loudly as if she knew she was going home. I didn't waste any time dressing her in the clothes I bought from home, wrapping her in a blanket, and loading her up in her car

How do you stand on the Word of God when your legs of FAITH are Broken?

Brandy "BrandyWine" Rankins

seat. The minutes felt like hours as we waited for Brielle to be discharged. When it finally happened, I was speechless as the moment felt so surreal; I couldn't believe it had finally come. As we walked out the hospital with Brielle in hand, I was screaming "THANK YOU JESUS" for the miracle.

As the days passed by, Brielle began growing and wanting more and more milk. Initially, this made me nervous because I couldn't stand to hear my baby cry from being hungry, but I didn't want to make her sick by giving her more milk than what the doctor ordered. I called my Dad and asked him what he thought I should do. *"Sweetheart, if that baby is hungry, feed her. She has been deprived for seven months, shoot; you got some pie around there? If she want that give her some of that too",* he joked. *"But naw feed that baby, she's hungry so let her eat",* he finished. I added another ounce to Brielle's three ounces of milk ordered by her doctor and then I began to pray on what I was about to do. I specifically asked the Lord not to allow me to give her the milk if it was going to harm her and to just bless her body so that she could receive it. Then, against the doctor's discretion and strict rules they sent us home with...I fed her more milk. Before long, I began feeding her more and more milk despite the doctor's orders. I watched her body language and I let her tell me when she was full and satisfied.

Brielle came home with a lot of different diagnoses: Acid reflux, Short bowel syndrome, vitamin d deficiency, anemia, and on and on and on. I pled the Blood of Jesus over every one of them and continued to proclaim she was healed. We made arrangements with our Pastor to have Brielle christened before the church. Even though the doctors told us not to take Brielle until spring, I felt it was imperative to show everyone that God is still a keeper and a healer. He is still performing miracles, especially when you need them the most. There were some who didn't agree with me bringing Brielle out to have her christened, but my intensions were solely to glorify God, and He gave me a comfort in my spirit that it was ok to do. I've learned that it's vital to understand God's voice so that you can use divine wisdom when making very serious decisions. Many times, when God tells you to do something, people are not going to agree; but I've decided to be a God pleaser and NOT a people pleaser. Brielle was christened and there were so many people who came out to support her. I shared her story on several different social web sites, so there were many praying her through. It was amazing that there were people that I never even met who came out to show their love and support and, most of all, Bless God for what He did. I hollered and shouted all up and down the sanctuary in complete joy and gratefulness of what my Lord had done. I remember hearing a Pastor say "when God allows you to be publicly crucified in front of the world, he publicly resurrects you in front of the world too." I had been through so much in my life and many times the world got to see it. I still have people coming up to me telling me they saw Thomas and me on the news from when our car was stolen. I wanted to say to the local news reporter who covered that story and spent several minutes afterward making jokes about how he wished us seven years of good luck "are you tuning in to this?" To me, this was a moment where God elevated us and I just wanted to stay there and bask in it for as long as I could.

*How do you stand on the Word of God
when your legs of FAITH are Broken?*

Brandy "BrandyWine" Rankins

I shouted to God because he told me at the hospital that he brought me back to my place of pain to heal me, and he kept his promise. He took Brielle from such a state of sickness and healed her beyond anything that I could've imagined. I literally begged both times for God to heal Ramone and my mother, but that wasn't His will. I believe it wasn't his will to heal Ramone and my mother here on earth; but give them a divine healing in Heaven instead. Now, I understand what the Bible means when it says "no weapon formed against me shall prosper". Yes, the weapons will come, the storms of life will arise, jobs will be lost, finances will be challenged, people we love dearly will pass on, and though we can never imagine making it through such difficult situations, in God and only in GOD we can. I thought for many years I was cursed or maybe God allowed such trials to occur to me because HE didn't like me. I had spent so much time blaming myself that I didn't know honestly how to accept God's love. However, Him taking me through this storm and every other storm prior, made me realize HE got the victory and joy in bringing me out. God knew exactly what it would take to restore my FAITH and to restore me, and because he loves me...He did it. He didn't have to do it, but I am sure glad and forever grateful that he did. God not only heard my prayer...HE SAID YES TO IT. **HE KEPT HIS PROMISE.**

How do you stand on the Word of God
when your legs of FAITH are Broken?

Brandy "BrandyWine" Rankins

He Kept His Promise;

*How do you stand on the Word of God
when your legs of FAITH are Broken?*

Brandy "BrandyWine" Rankins

He Kept His Promise;

Don't Let The Devil Win!
(When God delivers you from the hand of the enemy, your response is to "WORSHIP HIM")

{Declaration and Prayer}

- 235 -

*How do you stand on the Word of God
when your legs of FAITH are Broken?*

Brandy "BrandyWine" Rankins

He Kept His Promise;

On August 17, 2009, the day that I started writing the tenth chapter of this book, I received the news that I was having a miscarriage. I had just found out a few weeks earlier I was pregnant with our fifth child. I had been both spotting and lightly cramping for about a week before I had my first doctor's appointment. I called throughout the week to notify them of my spotting but they told me not to worry because some women bleed during their pregnancy and it was absolutely harmless.

When I first found out I was pregnant, it was an absolute shock, for it wasn't planned. We already had the four who are very young and our hands just seemed so full. Immediately, I felt shameful because, once again, here I was pregnant with no degree and, even though I'm married, I just felt like "the lady with all those children." The pregnancy brought out much insecurity that I had deeply hidden. More than ever, I did the one thing I've always fought hard not to do...care what others think of me.

You won't believe that, when I was about six months pregnant with Brielle, I had someone come up to me at church and say *"Dag, ya'll don't know how to have sex by now without having all those babies".* I was flabbergasted because she is older and it was during our welcome song where everyone goes around and meets and greets one another. Then there was the "dag, you pregnant again" or "you really got your hands full" remarks I'd get when I would simply be out at the store. Since when did it become okay for people to just give you their unasked for opinions? Well, this pregnancy definitely became different.

How do you stand on the Word of God
when your legs of FAITH are Broken?

Brandy "BrandyWine" Rankins

I was taught that, when you become a teacher for the Kingdom, the enemy will test you on the very thing that you teach. I definitely have found this to be the case time and time again since I have started speaking out and writing books. In my first book, I wrote: *"I had a choice to either give up or seek God like never before and get all that He has for me".* Since I've written that book, I have faced many tests that have put me in that same exact situation…either give up or seek God like never before and get all that He has for me. This chapter is an example of that. I don't want you to assume that, just because God brought me through one extreme and gave me a powerful testimony; the enemy isn't still attacking me. He is, and I say to you today my friends

"DON'T LET THE DEVIL WIN! WHEN THE LORD DELIVERS YOU FROM THE HAND OF THE ENEMY, YOUR RESPONSE IS TO WORSHIP HIM!"

My husband and I didn't know where the finances would come from to care for another child and surely we didn't have the room in the house for another baby, but we knew God was going to have to provide all of our need according to His riches in Glory. We prayed, and God began to encourage us through His word. We read a text of scripture where God said He was bringing us into good land and how the trials were only humbling us. (I'm Brandynizing this and not writing it verbatim) It said that He was doing this so that, when He elevated us, we would know that it was Him alone who did it; not money, people, or luck. I don't believe in luck anyway. I don't even believe things just happen by chance; I believe they are ordained by God.

- 237 -

The more we read, the more excited we became. I heard the name Brook in the scripture and told my husband I wanted to name the baby Brooke; we hoped it was a girl. With each passing day, we became so excited about Brooke. We told the kids about her and we fell in love with the idea that Brielle would have a sister to play with. I stopped being so self-conscious and, any opportunity I got, whether it was amongst friends or doing a speaking engagement; I began sharing with many the news of my pregnancy.

As I stated earlier, my spotting started around my ninth week. I don't have any insurance so I became a patient at a local women's clinic that helps pregnant women. Although they said not to worry about the bleeding, still in the back of my mind it bothered me to know I was spotting when I never spotted during any of my other pregnancies.

It was at my appointment that I received the news about the miscarriage. Once the nurse began going over all of my symptoms in detail, she was sure this was what I was experiencing. Instantly, I broke down into tears right there in front of the nurse. Just when I had become so excited about having a baby, it was being taken away. "I'm so upset because, in the beginning, I didn't want to be pregnant again. I was thinking I have four small children at home and what am I going to do with another", I ranted. "But never did I want anything to happen to my baby...I feel so terrible", I cried. "No Brandy, what you had was a normal reaction to an unplanned pregnancy", the nurse said. However, my conviction ran deeper because of my initial reaction. I felt like I have been through enough in my life and I should've just trusted God from the beginning.

The next day, I was scheduled for an ultrasound and it was confirmed that there was no heartbeat. No insecurity and no person's opinion mattered in the moments that I received that news. From there, I was told I would have to get a D&C, which is a medical procedure where you are put to sleep; a breathing tube is administered and the deceased baby is removed. I prayed against getting it done. I didn't want to be put to sleep, and the breathing tube made me uncomfortable, but again I knew I had to "trust God".

Within two weeks, I was rushed to the emergency room where I experienced a natural miscarriage. I saw more blood leave my body than I have ever seen in my life, and the experience was traumatic, yet through it all I kept saying "Lord I trust you, Lord I bless you". The enemy kept trying to feed doubts into my mind but I didn't receive it! Even as I sit here on my couch, two and half weeks after the miscarriage on bed rest, I type these words to you...**DON'T LET THE DEVIL WIN!** This book is written to encourage you to allow His anointing to break the strongholds and ungodly yokes in your life. The devil is trying to defeat you and I pray you will join me in declaring he is a liar! I dare you right now to stop what you are doing and acknowledge that every low place of your life is preparing you for your high place in Jesus! I challenge you to open your mouth and proclaim that abortion didn't break you, not even the backbiters, backstabbers, or the so called friends who abandoned you. So what your finances are being challenged! They may have repossessed your car, foreclosed your house, and

*How do you stand on the Word of God
when your legs of FAITH are Broken?*

Brandy "BrandyWine" Rankins

even fired you from your job, and still they couldn't steal your joy. You see, the world didn't give you joy and the world can't take it away; joy comes from the Lord. Happiness is based on what happens and I don't know about you but I can't afford to be on some rollercoaster of emotions based on what's happening; no I want God's joy!

That drug addiction, divorce, or domestic violence relationship that you just decided to reach up and grab the strength from God to leave didn't break you. You've been beat up, walked on, ran over, bruised, and many times half standing, but through Jesus you have the victory; don't you give up now. I don't care how scarce the economy is reporting your finances to be; the workforce is not your source-God is your source and I speak your cup not only full but running over. Touch and agree with me as we bind anxiety, panic attacks, low self-esteem, suicidal thoughts, depression, mental illnesses, prostitution, and molestation in Jesus` name. You may be afflicted in your body, but I don't care what the doctor is reporting-believe the report of the Lord. You've read my testimony and my story about Brielle, now I encourage you to take the DVD in the back of this book and watch it. See for yourself how God is still performing miracles and how much He loves you, how God is still a healer, a way maker, provider...truly He is the **"I AM"** of your every need. God is everywhere, but he is nowhere if you don't meet Him somewhere.

Now to Him who is able to do exceedingly abundantly above all that we ask or think, according to the power that works in us, Ephesians 3:20

How do you stand on the Word of God
when your legs of FAITH are Broken?

Brandy "BrandyWine" Rankins

Now is the time- it's time for you to get your healing and restoration. For some of you, it's time to finally confront your past just as I did. The enemy is warring to keep you bound to your past, but the decision is up to you. I have seen the enemy use people in an attempt to tell my story but can't NO DEVIL IN HELL tell MY story better than me. The enemy wants to shame you to silence, but when you receive the courage to tell it, he's ashamed because the chains of bondage literally break. Some of you have been living in the rear view mirrors of life for a long time but God is calling you to drive looking through the windshield. There are so many wonderful treasures He wants to show you here in the now. There is prosperity, abundance, and promise in your future, so why is your mind still stuck back in Egypt years after God already brought you out? The Bible talks about how our best days are ahead of us. This means "THE BEST IS YET TO COME"!

LADIES- I need to speak into my ladies for a minute, especially the young ones. I have a verse in one of my poems that says: *"It's time to tell these misguided young females to remove the price tags off of your priceless bodies. Yes, men's wallets can buy you nice expensive things but HIV is both non-refundable and non-returnable"*. Ladies your body is your temple. This is where the spirit of God dwells, which means it should be a sacred and holy place until you are married. Yes, I made the mistake of having sex before marriage but I don't want you to go through what I did- it's not worth it. These are soul ties you are making with these men. Sexually, you are making these men your husbands, yet some of you complain about not having a husband. How can God send you a husband when you already have many? It's absolutely

How do you stand on the Word of God
when your legs of FAITH are Broken?

Brandy "BrandyWine" Rankins

devastating to do this and then years later receive the revelation that you were bed hopping because you were looking for love and didn't really even know how to love yourself. For some, this word is going to cut and offend but I would like to save you the heartbreak and brokenness this road leads to. You shouldn't have to repeat many of the same mistakes I've made; I've gone through them for us both and that should be enough. Five years from now, will this man or any of the men you are fornicating with be your husband, or just another name lost in the alphabet soup of men that you've given your body to? You are a queen destined for greatness and God has not given just any man permission to enter your body. You are special, and both fearfully and wonderfully made God says.

I saw a documentary that showed how common it is for our young girls to have oral sex; they referred to it as "the new kiss good night." Mothers, Grandmothers, Sisters, Aunts, and God-mothers, what is happening to our young women? When do we say to the enemy 'ENOUGH" in regard to our daughters? Fathers, Grandfathers, Brothers, Uncles, and God-fathers, when do we say "ENOUGH" about our young men killing one another and dying in these streets to senseless violence? Since when did it become okay for someone to get stabbed to death because of an argument? When did it become okay for someone to get shot in the head because someone lost a fist fight? And when did it become okay for youth to take a loaded gun into our schools and shoot everyone in sight because of self-esteem issues? It's not okay and now is the time I need you to stand with me and say to the enemy "ENOUGH" and we will NOT let you have our children.

*How do you stand on the Word of God
when your legs of FAITH are Broken?*

Brandy "BrandyWine" Rankins

He Kept His Promise;

For believers, it's time to stop being weary and doubtful and start walking in total faith in the Lord, His Word, and His promises. I don't care what the doctor is reporting about your health-**BE HEALED!** It's time to stop mourning the death of that loved one in your life. You've become so heavy from carrying the hurt, depression, and anger so long that it's turned you into this bitter and miserable person. We will never understand the "why's" of God. His Word says His ways are higher than our ways and His thoughts are higher than our thoughts. Do you think your loved one wants you to carry the burden of their death while they are in Heaven enjoying eternal life? No, it's not fair that they had to go but there is ONE who can anoint your wounds and give you peace beyond understanding... His name is Jesus! Won't you allow Him to touch your wounds today? Today is the day of release. You didn't buy this book by happenstance- this was a DIVINE acquisition.

Repeat these words out loud to yourself: "I will make it, I will NOT give up!" I don't care how dark your past is or how sinister you feel your sin is-God is the remedy! It doesn't even matter how long you have been in bondage or whether or not you have attended church yet- today is the day you are coming out because God says so!

The Lord is not slack concerning his promise, as some men count slackness; but is longsuffering toward us, not willing that any should perish, but that all should come to repentance. <u>2 Peter 3:9</u> (King James Version)

*How do you stand on the Word of God
when your legs of FAITH are Broken?*

Brandy "BrandyWine" Rankins

As far as Brielle- well why don't you see on the next page for yourself?! This is her today! Many of her diagnoses don't even remain and I know God is going to finish the good work he started in her. Today she is one years old and she's both walking and talking. She's still on special milk but she just about eats everything she can get her tiny fingers on. When she sees herself on the DVD, she's puts her head back and extends her arms in worship. Some of her first words were "thank you Jesus, hallelujah, Daddy, and Glory".

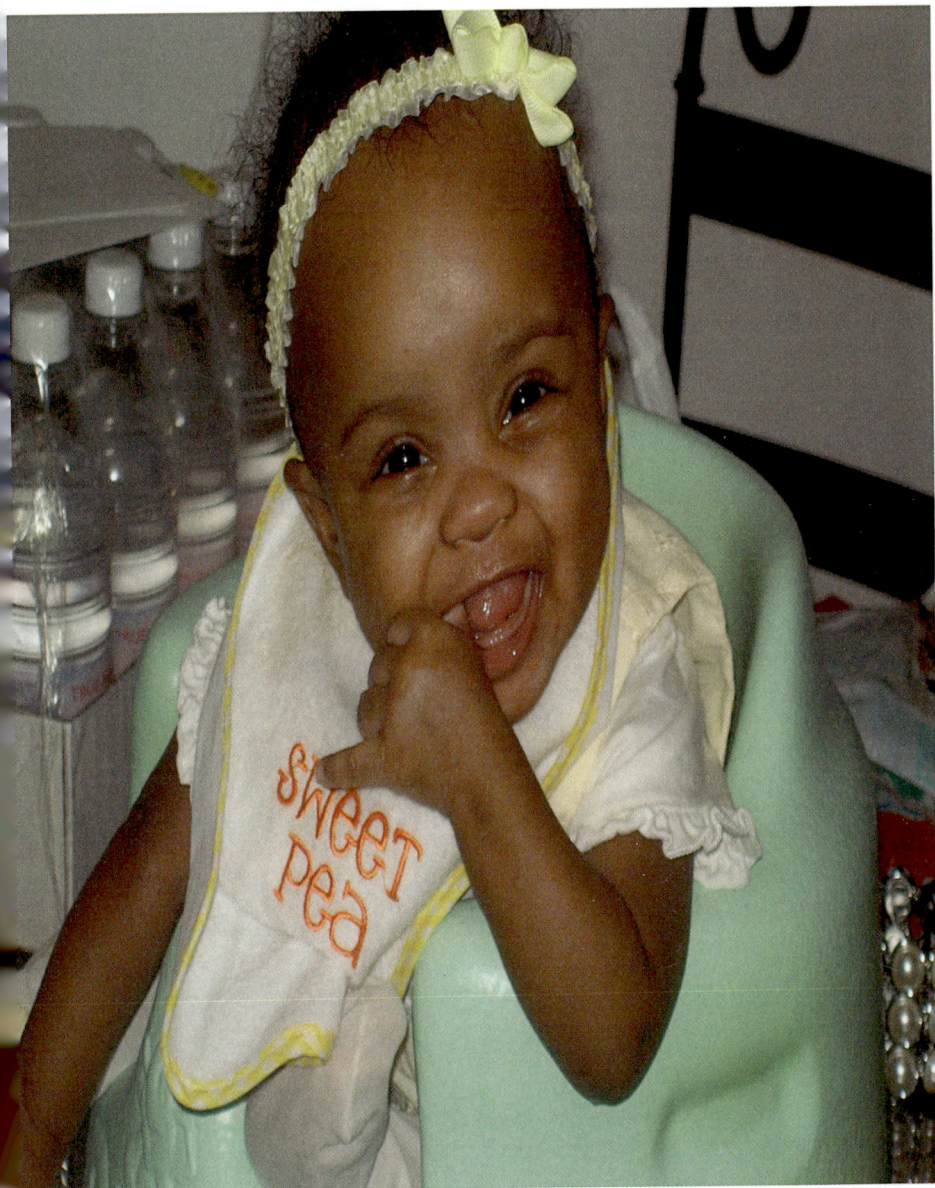

How do you stand on the Word of God
when your legs of FAITH are Broken?

Brandy "BrandyWine" Rankins

He Kept His Promise;

Somebody has been waiting on a miracle from God and this book is going to be a tool He uses to speak to them in a mighty way. It's for that very reason alone that every sweat, tear, and obstacle of my testimony was worth hurdling over so that God could be glorified and bless you. Not only is He a keeper of His Word but...

HE KEPT HIS PROMISE!
How do you stand on the Word of God when your legs of FAITH are broken? <u>By allowing God to HEAL your brokenness and restore you</u>; just look at what HE did for me!

*How do you stand on the Word of God
when your legs of FAITH are Broken?*

Brandy "BrandyWine" Rankins

- 247 -

How do you stand on the Word of God
when your legs of FAITH are Broken?

Brandy "BrandyWine" Rankins

He Kept His Promise;

*How do you stand on the Word of God
when your legs of FAITH are Broken?*

Brandy "BrandyWine" Rankins

May the Lord, the God of your fathers, make you a thousand times as many as you are and bless you as He has promised you!

~Deuteronomy 1:11 (Amplified Bible)

Many people believe that Hell is not real. In fact, many believe "since I'm a good person, I'm going to heaven". However, that's not what the Bible says. Do you think that being a good person is enough to get you into Heaven? I invite you to take the short quiz below to see just how "good" of a person you are.

1) Have you ever disrespected your parents?
2) Have you ever committed adultery?
3) Have you ever stolen something?
4) Have you ever coveted or wanted something that belonged to someone else? (I.E. money, a car, house, wife, husband, etc)
5) Have you ever taken the Lord's name in vain?
6) Have you ever murdered?
7) Have you ever worked all seven days of the week instead of putting aside the seventh day to worship the Lord?
8) Have you ever put anything or anyone before the Lord, making them your god?
9) Have you ever wrongfully accused someone?
10) Have you ever made for yourself a carved image or any likeness of anything that is in Heaven above or the Earth beneath and bowed down to it?

**Okay, now its time to see how you did. Did you answer yes to any of these ten questions? Of course you did. And it is by your own admission alone that you are guilty. So, what do you do? Jesus is the only solution to your problem. You need salvation through Jesus. The Bible says that liars, adulterers, etc have no place in the

Kingdom of God. But you don't want to spend your eternity in Hell either do you? Of course you don't and you don't have to. Why not a religion other than Christianity? (i.e. Buddhism, Jehovah's Witness, Muslim, etc.) Christianity is the only religion that tells us there is **no** other **name under heaven** given among men, whereby we must be saved. (Acts 4:12). It also tells us that, because Jesus died on the cross for our sins, we can have eternal life. Finally, it tells us that, unless we accept and believe Jesus to be our Lord and Savior, we cannot receive eternal life and be connected to God the Father. **Take a look**.

That as sin hath reigned unto death, even so might grace reign through righteousness unto eternal life by Jesus Christ our Lord. Romans 5:21 (King James Version)

23For the wages of sin is death; but the gift of God is eternal life through Jesus Christ our Lord. Romans 6:23 (King James Version)

20And we know that the Son of God is come, and hath given us an understanding, that we may know him that is true, and we are in him that is true, even in his Son Jesus Christ. This is the true God, and eternal life. 1 John 5:20 (King James Version)

6Jesus saith unto him, I am the way, the truth, and the life: no man cometh unto the Father, but by me. John 14:6 (King James Version)

Many will hear God's Good News (The Gospel) and reject it. But what about you, are you ready to receive salvation?

If you have never accepted Jesus Christ as your Lord and Savior, you can do so today by simply doing the following:

1) Confess that you are a sinner and admit your need (Lord I have done...)
2) Be willing to turn away from your sins/ wrongful doings (Repent)
3) Believe that Jesus died on the cross for you and on the third day rose from the grave.
4) Ask Jesus through prayer to come into your heart and be in control of your life.
5) Be Baptized of the water and the Spirit (Re-birth)
6) Accept Him as your Lord and Savior!

It's just that easy! If you have followed these simple steps right now, then the Bible says you are saved.

Romans 10:8-10 (Amplified Bible)

[8]But what does it say? The Word (God's message in Christ) is near you, on your lips and in your heart; that is, the Word (the message, the basis and object) of faith which we preach, [A]

[9]Because if you acknowledge and confess with your lips that Jesus is Lord and in your heart believe (adhere to, trust in, and rely on the truth) that God raised Him from the dead, you will be saved.

[10]For with the heart a person believes (adheres to, trusts in, and relies on Christ) and so is justified (declared righteous, acceptable to God), and with the mouth he confesses (declares openly and speaks out freely his faith) and confirms [his] salvation.

[5]Jesus answered, Verily, verily, I say unto thee, Except a man be born of water and of the Spirit, he cannot enter into the kingdom of God. **John 3:5 (King James Version)**

How do you stand on the Word of God when your legs of FAITH are Broken?

Brandy "BrandyWine" Rankins

<u>*My Sincere Thanks*</u>

Lord first and foremost all my thanks, praise, honor and glory goes to you. Truly you are the Head of my life concerning all things and I just thank you for never leaving me and for giving me the strength and anointing to share my testimony. Now I know what it means to have a relationship with you. I no longer live in fear because you are teaching me how to cast all of my cares on you. I love you. To my wonderful, anointed, and fine Kingdom Husband Thomas~ I love you and I thank God for you. Truly you are my partner concerning ALL things; thank you for always being my best friend. To my beautiful and precious babies~ Jah'Mir, Toma'rez, Braelyn, and Brielle: I love you all so very, very much. You guys have sacrificed a lot of time just so that I could even write this book-Thank you. Thank you all for loving me and giving me strength at the worst of times and at the best times. I am and will always be so proud of you! You are the best babies in the whole world and truly we are the best family! Mommy loves you always! Bishop C. Wayne Brantley and First Lady Brantley~ Thank you for being such powerful mentors and spiritual parents in my life. You have affirmed me with tools I will use for eternity. I hope you and our church are proud-love you. Lady Linda Lipford~ You are such an Awesome woman of God and I love you so much. You have been there for me in ways that mean so much to me. I can always call you for prayer, encouragement, and I just thank God that no matter how bad the storms of life get I know I always have a friend I can call on. You have been a mother, sister, grandmother, aunt, mentor and beyond to my family and me. I pray you have been inspired to share your own story because truly your testimony is powerful~ I

*How do you stand on the Word of God
when your legs of FAITH are Broken?*

Brandy "BrandyWine" Rankins

love you. To the entire Zion Pentecostal Church of Christ family~ I love you! To my Diddy~ Thank you for all of your hard work by helping edit this book. This has been a new season for us to really get to know one another and I thank God that you are my Dad. I love you always and unconditionally. Senequa~ Thank you for always having my back and being there when I needed you most. You have always been a wonderful sister and I thank you for the sacrifices you have made time and time again to support me. You are not just my sister you are my friend and I cherish the relationship we share. I love you and there is nothing but greatness inside of you. Jodi~ I love you and miss you very much. I am and will always be so proud of you and I know you will conquer your dreams. I pray God's blessings upon you and yours. Akil~ I miss you sooooooo much. Please know that no matter what I love you and I'm always here whenever you need me. I am so very proud of you! Chanse, Sage, and Jeremiah~ You are my babies and I love you all! Always follow your dreams they really do come true. Eric~ Thank you for always being there and being such a wonderful big brother and friend. You are never more than a phone call away and I thank God for you. I am so very proud of you and can't wait to see all of the wonderful things God has in store for you. This is YOUR season! Andrea~ Thank you for being my sister and friend. It means the world to me that you jumped in your car and drove three hours to see about me when some locally didn't even stop by or pick up the phone to call. It blesses me to know God loves me so much that he's sent me people like you. Thank you for loving my brother and for simply being ordained as everything that He needs. I love you and I am so excited about this wonderful journey as a family we will share. God bless your mom, dad, sister, and entire family. Jared~ Thank you for simply being you. You are my

*How do you stand on the Word of God
when your legs of FAITH are Broken?*

Brandy "BrandyWine" Rankins

coach, mentor, inspiration, realist, and most of all my big brother. You have always been there for me, no matter the hour or distance. You told me to get free however I needed to get free and finally I am-THANK YOU. Lisa~ My sister, my counselor, confidante, and very close friend. I woke you up at 5am for help and you didn't complain one bit, thank you for always having a heart for me. I have and can talk to you about anything and you are always there to listen and guide me through. Many times I complain to you about who's not in my life but today I focus on all the wonderful blessings in my life; like you. Many times I wish you and Jared lived closer but I know you're never more than a phone call away. I love you! Chas~ I love you and miss you dearly. I am so proud of you. To all my wonderful nieces and nephews~ I love you and pray this book blesses you beyond imagination. Bobby Gist~ One of my favorite cousins I thank God for you. Thank you for always loving and supporting me like a genuine cousin. I know we are in laws but you have never treated me that way. Thank you for simply being you. We love you, Lee Lee, and the boys! Auntie Boosie & Uncle Vince~ Thank you for being you. You have always been so genuine and I appreciate it. You have been supportive and most of all you have loved me unconditionally. I love you and Lil Vince always! Kourtney~ I LOVE YOU MANNN! LOL. I am so proud of you cousin and thank God for you. You and Jeremy are in my prayers always. To Lisa and Chip Parker~ Mom and Pop thank you for being such blessings in my life. Mom thanks for always supporting my books and selling them at any family function you could; it meant the world to me. Kisha~ Thank you for being such a wonderful sister and keeping the kids for us when we needed it most. I am so proud of you, your business, and just maintaining everyday as a strong woman. I know it's not easy

*How do you stand on the Word of God
when your legs of FAITH are Broken?*

Brandy "BrandyWine" Rankins

but God has so much in store for you- I love you. Tonya~ I send my deepest condolences about Buddy. I definitely know what it's like to lose someone you love. I pray you finish your book because there is a world waiting to read it. Please know I'm always here for you, whenever you need. Net~ I love you and we really are gonna have to get together more. I am so proud of you and be excited about walking in what God has in store for you~IT'S MIRACULOUS! Nee Nee and Tash~ I love you and hope we can strengthen our relationship as sisters. LaMar~ I love you and support you in all things. Aunt Patricia & Uncle William, Alisha, Shantelle, Aunt Betty & Uncle Roger, Trinita, LaToya, Tiniya, Quincy, Uncle Donald, Aunt Jean & Joan, Aunt Donna & Towanda, Aunt Brenda, Uncle Slim, Makia, and my ENTIRE FAMILY- I LOVE YOU ALWAYS and thank you for your unconditional support! Shaun~You are my best and closest friend, my sister, beautician, nail tech, and beyond. What can I say? You are the Robin to my Batman, the Jonathan to my David, the Ruth to my Naomi, and in all things I know you got my back. From my mother's passing to the miscarriage you have been right there by my side literally, whether it's in the hospital chair all night or sitting in the waiting room until 6 in the morning. Some search their entire life looking for a true friend and I'm so blessed that God gave me you. I love you so much and I'm so honored to have you in my life. You are an excellent wife, mother, and friend; truly an Awesome Woman of God. I love you and believing God for your miracle. Scott~ thank you for not only being a wonderful friend and role model to my husband but to me as well. You have gone above and beyond the call to be there for my family and me and truly I thank you. Thank you for your hard work in helping edit this book...words can't even express my gratitude. Quiana & Isaiah ~ Thank you for all the *help this summer. I am so blessed to have God children like you both. Quiana continue being a leader and standing out; the in crowd cannot handle your anointing. Isaiah I'm watching you in school now- continue to make us proud. Kia ~ Thank you for always making yourself available to me, being a friend, and praying me through. I thank God for genuine friends like you. I love you! Minister Nickens and Deacon Nickens ~ Thank you for your unconditional love and support especially at some of the darkest times of my life. We love you! Sister Lisa Womack and family~ Thank you for being a spiritual mom to me. Your love, kindness, and support have always meant the world. Thank you for keeping the kids for us, we will never take your kindness for granted. We love you! Antonise Harris~ My very first friend that I met when I was four what can I say? Truly I love you and thank God for you. No matter how far you have ALWAYS been here for me, always. Every wedding, funeral, and birth- you've been there and I thank you! Follow your dreams and know that we are NEVER too old to see them come true. I love you! Tamika~ My second friend I thank God for you and reuniting us. I am so excited about your book and can't wait until it hits stores. To your mother I love you dearly and I love your children more. God bless you and Shawn in all things!~ More than I can say I love you and THANK YOU for offering yourself to me-THAT IS THE LOVE OF GOD! And I will be over*smile* Shantelle~ Girl, book two!! Can you even believe it!? I just thank God for you. You have been my prayer partner, motivator, and such a wonderful friend. You have spoken life into me when I needed it most. During the miscarriage you not only came by and took care of my children, but you washed my dishes, and took care of me...wow I know that's God. You are an anointed Minister and you are right you do have a lot of ministry to pour out on people;*

just look at how you've poured into me. I love you and thank you for loving and always supporting me. Darnell~ Thank you for being such a great friend to my husband and me. Truly you know the meaning of service and sacrifice and I'm honored to call you and your wife friend. Uriah and Darnell Jr.~ I love you. James~ you have always been my brother and one of husband's closest friends. Thank you for always listening (because you know we can both talk-smile) and being supportive. You have seen first hand the many storms God has brought me and Boo through and I thank God for your friendship, fellowship, and love. We love you always! Ministers Ida and Michael Wells~ Thank you for ALWAYS being here for us. We love you so much and will never forget your acts of kindness, love, and friendship that you have shown towards us. You will always be our family. We love you! Tracy~ I love you and Frost very much! I'm so excited about your wedding and thank you for always supporting me and being a kingdom example. The enemy has been attacking you so much because he knows he cannot stop your destiny. I love you Tira (F.R.E.E.)~ Thank you for always being supportive of my dreams. God has placed so much power and an authority inside of you, I can't wait for you to really see it. You have provided me with the tools I needed to even write and publish my books-I love you, Tam (Unek) I love you and my niece always! Jahna~ I thank God for you! You are so funny and intelligent but most of all, my friend. Remember your inheritance from God through your mother-the will says you are RICH! RICH IN SPIRIT, RICH IN PROSPERITY, AND MOST OF ALL RICH IN MENTAL HEALTH. Thank you for coming over and helping me when I needed it most- I will never forget that. I love you. Delecia~ Thank you for being such a wonderful friend to me. You have always been someone I could confide in and my sister. I know you have my back in all things because you always have-thank you and I love you. Shawana~ Thank you for always looking out for me and my family. We love you and Kayla. Special shout outs to Latisha Davis~ I love you and thank you! Daphne~ I love you and thank God for bringing you into my life. Harriet~ God brought you and your children back into my life when I needed it most. Thank you for just being so down to earth and the loving person you are. You have been so supportive and it means the world. You have reminded me so many times who I am in CHRIST and I-thank you and I love you for it! Tanya~ Thank you for the love and kindness you and your family have shown me. Thank you for inviting me to speak at your church and for the wonderful fellowship. I feel like I can talk to you about anything-thank you for being so down to earth. I love you! Pastor Marilyn~ Thank you for the love, support, and for allowing me to speak at your church-it blessed me abundantly. I love you! Traci "Chrissy" Brown~ Isn't God awesome in how he will use us? God not only sent you for Healthy Start but He has allowed us to minister to each other on several occasions. You are a wonderful person and remember what God has for you is for you! Anitra~Thank you for being my big sister. You have always been so supportive and prayerful for Brielle and my entire family when you have a lot on your own plate. May the Lord bless you more abundantly than you have blessed me. Pastor Mike~ Thank you for allowing to me come to both of your churches in PA and share my testimony. More than I can say it blessed me for you to turn over your pulpit to me before you even met me-thank you for trusting God! Marti, Allen, Cagney~ Thank you for the love and for opening up your home to us. Thank you for inviting me all the way to PA to tell my testimony. I love you all and thank you for making us feel like family. Sis Precious~ Thank you for the unconditional love and

How do you stand on the Word of God
when your legs of FAITH are Broken?

Brandy "BrandyWine" Rankins

support and for promoting my books on your radio show. Minister Bailey~Thank you for speaking this book into my life! We love you! Minister Jackson~ Awesome Woman of God, what else can I say besides I love you. If I need a word from God I know where to come. You have always been a wonderful friend and someone I could talk to. For everything-thank you! Asia & Joseph James~ special blessings and love to your family. Special thanks to Sherman"LS Royal" Stewart- it means the world to me to have you apart of my book on the blurb. I'm honored to have you do a review. You are my brother and have encouraged me to reach for my dreams-thank you! Special Thanks to Lady Linda Lipford, Pastor Marilyn Harp, Bobby Gist, Pastor Mike Benner, and Marti Brown. To all of my aunts, uncles, cousins, and family I love you and thank you for your unconditional love and support! Thank you for every Pastor that has invited me to speak.

To anyone I may have forgotten, please charge it to my head and not my heart! God bless and I Love you

How do you stand on the Word of God when your legs of FAITH are Broken?

Brandy "BrandyWine" Rankins

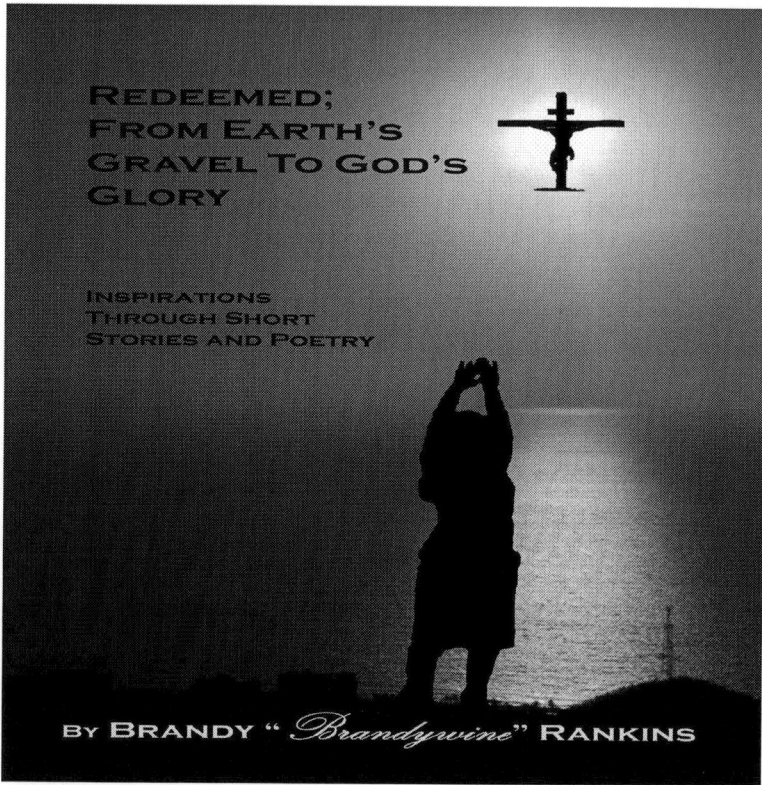

REDEEMED;
FROM EARTH'S
GRAVEL TO GOD'S
GLORY

INSPIRATIONS
THROUGH SHORT
STORIES AND POETRY

BY BRANDY " *Brandywine*" RANKINS

If you enjoyed this book you will also love my first book!

Visit www.freewebs.com/brandywine01

*How do you stand on the Word of God
when your legs of FAITH are Broken?*

Brandy "BrandyWine" Rankins

Check out this anointed album by Da Answer at:
www.daanswer.webs.com

How do you stand on the Word of God
when your legs of FAITH are Broken?

Brandy "BrandyWine" Rankins

The Redeemed Newsletter

JULY 2009

Sealed The Deal
By: Mrs. Kellie Jackson

Mrs. Kellie Jackson

"The word of the Lord came to me saying, "Before I formed you in the womb I knew you..." (Jeremiah 1:4-5)

These very important words were spoken to the prophet Jeremiah before he accepted the call on his life. We as believers should all hear a personal invite, an intimate message from God that remains with us for a lifetime. Just as a business man places his John Hancock on a contract to make it binding. God places his mark on everything and everybody that belongs to him. There is no guessing when it comes to God, He always "seals the deal". Be encouraged as I share with you

a piece of my testimony about how God sealed the deal in my life.

Imagine an 18 year old girl coming to the alter to meet her savior. A slave to sin, she's burdened with heavy metal shackles on her hands and feet. She, who once thought it was cool to be out partying at all times of the night, keeping company with drug dealers, smoking and drinking, is now left scarred from the experience of the streets. Vivid memories of unfortunate events visit her once again: like the time she thought she would never make it home after being kidnapped and taken advantage of. "Was it God who told her when and where to run to, to make it to safety?" she thought to herself. "Ok. Well, God was that you who kept me from running into someone I wanted to kill when I had that gun in my hand?" "But God you saw what he did to me! I looked like a monster after being assaulted with that rock!" "You really should have let me have my way with him!" She heard, "Vengeance is mine. Is he not paying for it now? Do you think that these people can look at you and tell what you've been through? I was unrecognizable when the people

tortured and crucified me! But I loved them anyhow! Just come my child, I have the answers for all of your questions, healing for all of your pain." She suddenly felt a sense of urgency to reach the alter as tears rolled down her cheeks. She begins to see a glimpse of hope as the light shines bright at the end of the pitchy tunnel. By the time she reaches the preacher, she has already accepted Jesus into her heart. She has already felt the shackles being broken from her feet. She now knows that she can walk right out of the pain and into her Savior's loving arms. She can now lift her hands in praise and adoration because now the shackles have been broken from her hands. "What a love, what a rush, what an experience! How can people go through life without this mind blowing, breathtaking encounter?" she thought. " So how", you might ask, "did God seal the deal in your life?" I begin to question what just happened to me. "Was it real?" I began to ask myself. I remember the preacher asking God

to seal up my confession until the day of redemption. As I took my seat, I began to wonder how God was going to "seal it up". I left church a little confused. My best friend Yolonda tried to help me sort through some of my confusion as she went home with me that night. After all, she had run the streets with me and now we were both starting a new life. But even she could not convince me that my encounter with God was not based solely on emotion. As I went to sleep that night I heard a still, small, crystal clear voice saying, "four corners...

(CONTINUED ON PAGE 2)

Inside this issue:

SEALED THE DEAL	1
LIFE'S BATTLES...	2&3
The Prodigal	4-8
CONTACT US	9

How do you stand on the Word of God when your legs of FAITH are Broken?

Brandy "BrandyWine" Rankins

He Kept His Promise;

Remembering and Honoring

The memory of

Those We Love.

My Mom the late Sharon Ann Poteat, the late Mr. Bill Cooper, the late Mr. Kevin "Buddy" Martin, the late Mr. Robert James King Sr., the late Mr. Theopolis Heard, the late Ms. Simplicity Johnson, the late Auntie Blanche "Cheeny" Coburn, and the late Dianne Harris.

How do you stand on the Word of God when your legs of FAITH are Broken?

Brandy "BrandyWine" Rankins

Final Remarks

Last, I just wanted to say that, while this book reflects my actual testimony, the events, the pain, and the people are a thing of the past. The way anyone has mistreated me through the events of this book happened yesterday. Today, I pray that all individuals are changed and have found both salvation and prosperity in the Lord. I do not hold an ought against anyone portrayed in this book; and my purpose in both writing and distributing this book is solely to GLORIFY GOD. It is my hope that many who read this book will become saved and those already saved will become encouraged.

Finally, I ask and pray that, if anyone portrayed in this book is holding an ought against me, please forgive me and release me from your spirit the same as I have already released you. I am not the same person I used to be and, today, God not only has me positioned in "**GREATNESS**" but I am walking in it. The only person I'm out to destroy is the devil and he is already defeated in Jesus' name!

If you haven't already viewed it, please watch the DVD included with this book and share it with others. God bless you always and again thank you for sowing into this ministry!

Respectfully,

Brandy "*BrandyWine*" Rankins